The Hidden Agenda

THE WILEY MANAGEMENT SERIES ON PROBLEM SOLVING, DECISION MAKING, AND STRATEGIC THINKING

The Hidden Agenda

RECOGNIZING WHAT REALLY MATTERS AT WORK

PRISCILLA ELFREY

JOHN WILEY & SONS

New York   Chichester   Brisbane   Toronto   Singapore

82192

Library of Congress Cataloging in Publication Data

Elfrey, Priscilla, 1932–
      The hidden agenda.

      (Wiley management series on problem solving, decision
making, and strategic thinking)
      Bibliography: p.
      Includes index.
      1. Management.   I. Title.   II. Series.
HD31.E548   1982   658   82-8500
ISBN   0-471-86529-X   AACR2

Printed in the United States of America

10 9 8 7 6 5 4

With love to
John
Kristen
Stephen
and my parents

Whatever you can do, or dream you can, begin it.
Boldness has genius, power and magic in it.

GOETHE

Preface

I wrote this book for executives and readers who are serious about meeting the country's current challenges in productivity, quality, and achievement. It is not a book that shows how to use less than desirable tactics to get ahead at work. It is about recognizing what really matters and coming to grips with the essentials of leadership. You can raise levels of achievement and strip away waste and inefficiency. This requires discipline, thought, and action, but I can do it and so can you. Those who concentrate on the main event can achieve their goals, learn to keep out of trouble, and become substantially different, more effective people.

Look through this book for help with your particular needs—defining your self-interest, cutting clutter, seeking solutions, developing your own career, selecting and developing others, telling your story, gathering support, persisting, and surviving. There is a discipline to my approach that you can discard or modify after you have learned it.

You, of course, have your own preferences and style and can break rules that do not work for you. Indeed, people say that leadership is about breaking rules. First, however, you must learn the rules. If you break them unconsciously, you can find yourself in trouble and not know why. If you know the rules and decide to break them anyway, you may get in trouble. You can, however, have contingency plans, and thus prepared, spare yourself surprises. You can learn—when something doesn't work—to do something else.

One of the purposes of this book is to enable you to eliminate unwelcome surprises. It starts with the premise that things almost certainly will go wrong. You needn't be a pessimist or try vainly to form foolproof plans. You must recognize that the forces fostering unproductiveness, wastefulness, discord, and chaos are formidable. Much of what is going on at work is hidden from us, even concealed or cloaked in secrecy. Mostly, however, the agenda is merely out of our immediate sight or right in front of us and unnoticed. If you don't ask yourself "What business am I in?," you may be unaware of your own hidden agenda.

As I began this book, I wrote "maybe," "in many cases," and "probably," over and over. I then decided on a more forthright approach. A book on leadership has to take risks. Any statements about management should be accompanied by qualifications. In my thoughts, they are always present, but on paper, they wreak havoc with style.

The Hidden Agenda is based on my experience, not in a laboratory or study, but in work places. It is a collection of management tools, stories, and approaches to achievement. It includes theories from management and other social sciences as well as ideas from the arts and literature. I am not as interested in theory and technique as I am in practical work that pays attention to what is going on. I have looked for effective procedures and practices and for simple reporting systems that explain in plain English what needs to be done, how, when, and by whom.

It would be easier to identify and act on the main event if we understood more about what works at work. We know surprisingly little about what managers do every day, how leaders achieve, and what, over the centuries, has distinguished the people who have gotten the world's work done. We act as if people instinctively know how to work. Our experience tells us otherwise. I know a man who earned an advanced degree in business administration from a renowned university. When we first met, he had held and lost more than twenty jobs. He told me that when he shaved every morning, he looked in the mirror and wondered how he would get through the day. He sent his secretary off to do "research." He moved papers, sat quietly at meetings, and hoped that nothing would go wrong. In the past two years, he has held three more jobs. He is now unemployed, perhaps permanently. Agony etches his face. His study of management has no connection with his work or life.

Many people say that they want to manage but are unable to concentrate on learning how. They are fascinated by the single-mindedness of leadership and attracted to what they perceive as the by-products—control, power, and money. Few recognize what really matters—discipline, detachment, and concentration. These qualities are difficult to maintain, but no one said that management would be easy. Self-interest is the key. Either we will become better leaders, or we will be finished.

Among those who have helped me understand what is important and to whom I am grateful are Marjorie Nichols, John Kouwenhoven, Lucyle Hook, Barry Ulanov, Robert Straus, Robert Brustein, Ray Smith, Martha Coigney, Martha Orrick, Sidney Lanier, Neil Postman, Gene Monick, Hannah Weiner, Dick Bolles, Horace Taft, Jack Embersits, John Crystal, my family, and colleagues in the Office of Management Development and Training and in the Career Advisory Service. They contributed an invaluable store of experiences. Those who encouraged and supported the writing of this book deserve special thanks: Jon Michael Smith, George Peabody, George and Stella Redfearn, Stephen Hartke, Delores Hart, Louis De Angelis, Hugh Harris, Helen Lambert, Mary Douglas, who typed the early chapters when I was in Annapolis, and Gail Larsen, who typed the final manuscript in Florida. My husband, John, and my daughter Kristen Hartke, have been wonderfully supportive. I owe much to them and am also grateful to Kristen for preparing the bibliography. They, more than anyone else, helped me every day to keep my eye on the main event.

PRISCILLA ELFREY

Cocoa Beach, Florida
June 1982

Contents

One

Know What to Do

One of the beautiful moments a coxswain has is when all eight oars are clicking at the same time. You don't always get all the divisions of a company clicking together but that's what you strive for.
THORNTON BRADSHAW

Keep your eye on the main event.
MARTHA GRIFFITHS

The main event is the principal point at stake. It is important. Making all the oars click at the same time involves knowing where your self-interest is, striving for excellence, getting out of trouble, and identifying and achieving goals. A lot of factors hamper this effort. Improved productivity eludes us. Everything takes longer. We blame the tax structure, inflation, regulations, aging factories, unions, politicians, lending institutions, the media, the educational system, and the family. Yet in January 1981, the *Wall Street Journal* reported that managers themselves "cite poor management as the key reason for lackluster productivity." Turning this around calls for courage and requires us to focus resources in compelling new ways. There are positive elements to be found in negative situations just as there are negative aspects of positive moments. It is difficult to remember that it is the needs of customers, clients, and constituents which drive well-managed organizations—not financial reports or management tools.

Managers operate largely by insight and feelings in an unstructured world. Understanding our own perspectives and values as well as those of our customers is not simple, especially when we find ourselves in the midst of whirling systems both inside and outside the organization.

Aiming for elegance in such a complex, messy, jumbled world sounds pretentious. Many problems are beyond our control and exogenous forces impede progress, so that it is no wonder that we find it easier to react than to act. Routine but necessary events vie for our time. We can see that if we do not eliminate the clutter, the clutter will eliminate us.

Conventional teaching about management, based on an idea of clear sequential planning and rational activity, offers little help. Chapters in textbooks and class lessons divide management neatly and unnaturally into planning, organizing, staffing, coordinating, reviewing, budgeting, and delegating. This in fact has little to do with getting the job done.

Today's work environments require new survival skills and new approaches. The traditional assumptions fail to work. We'd like to organize a championship team, start a new Silicon Valley, produce a *My Fair Lady*, or launch an Apollo 11. Yet, those times seem to be gone, and the practice of winning seems to be slip sliding away.

Everyone complains that things are getting worse. Solutions to problems beget worse problems. A new law destroys jobs, eliminates products, and creates side effects never envisioned by the planners. Regulations about personal responsibility for supervisory action cause managers to inquire about malpractice insurance. Minorities and women claim that opportunity is not equal, and white males complain that there is too much affirmative action.

Achieving results is so difficult that many of us have given up or are burned out. "Future Shock," which Alvin Tofler predicted would occur when we discover that the world we believe in no longer exists, is a daily "now shock." At the end of the week, we may wonder what we have accomplished. Few of us are doing as well as we think we are doing, and no one seems to care.

We sense that the clutter in our work is what creates crises and threatens to kill us. No one told us that management would be so messy, that failure to deal with change could be so dangerous. It is the principal thesis of this book that in order to meet the challenge of constantly accelerating change, we must find ways to concentrate on what is most important. We must keep our eyes on the main event.

The mark of a leader may be the ability to prevent fire fighting behavior and to seek elegant solutions. Elegance is, admittedly, seldom achieved, but many would make the effort. This book is, in part, about elegance, about achievement and results, about managing work by keeping the main event clearly in view. This sounds deceptively simple but it is not. Developing the abilities and attitudes to deal adequately with change—particularly those that appear to be negative—should be our highest priority. We need to distinguish between what is important and what is unimportant. We need to discover the undiscovered main event, to work out the problems that obscure the main event, and to deal with both the expected and the unexpected main event.

It is an illusion to think that innovation and improvement occur without our intervention. Our behavior is at the center of successful change.

Like most of us, I first learned this principle on the playing field, where my father would admonish me to keep my eye on the ball. At ten, I was the smallest member of my class and had no experience playing ball. I dreaded physical education, for no captains wanted me on their teams. The daily humiliation of being chosen last stiffened my resolve. Nightly practice under my father's tutelage made the difference. By keeping my eye on the ball and by concentrating on my swing, I became a consistent, if weak, hitter. Since I usually made it safely to first base, my value as a team player rose. This lesson followed me from golf to tennis to soccer to squash. Every time I lost my concentration, I expended energy trailing after the ball. I saw the application in college when, failing to clarify an assignment, I had to redo a major research project. At work there were other problems. Like Joan Didion's Maria Wyeth, I often did not know what the game was. This made it difficult to "play it as it lays." I struggled to understand the systems within systems. I learned that what should work usually did not, and that virtue was not rewarded. First, I had a difficult time even identifying which things really mattered. Then I had to learn to keep an eye on them.

The external forces that get in the way of mastering the game are formidable. Suspicion and fear block our paths. Competition, even between departments, creates barriers of defensiveness and mistrust. Sometimes staff offices are seen as enemies rather than as supports. Then, they will often behave as enemies. Corporate publications rarely give a hint about what is really important to the organization. In some companies, to avoid any chance of unpleasantness, employers tell employees nothing.

Mismanagement of time mars our lives. People we want to see are never in. Twenty-minute meetings take three hours. Then too, needed supplies are seldom in stock. I am reminded daily: "When you find something that you like, buy a lifetime supply. They are going to stop making it." Most of us work in places where a person who wants to block something has an easier route than a person who wants to accomplish something. There is often little concern for whether or not things are done. By action or inaction, anyone can cause work to stop or slow down. The rules and the style seem to be more important than the results. Activity is almost always confused with achievement.

The internal forces are even stronger. Walt Kelly tells us: "We have met the enemy and he is us." Our inconstancy of purpose, our inattention to detail, our undisciplined approach to planning, communication, and action, and our lack of courage make us wonder how we do as well as we do. More than one manager has told me the same story. They reach home at night and once inside, lean against the locked door. Each then breathes, "They didn't catch me today. I made it."

We shake our heads at the counterproductive behavior of our bosses, our peers, our subordinates, and ourselves. The pessimists tell us there is no hope. Charles Lindblom is convincing when he states that man can only make piecemeal efforts to wrestle "bravely with a universe that he is wise enough to know is too big for him." It seems as if we cannot really cope with the complexity. We never have enough information and seldom can control the timing of events or make realistic predictions. This causes most managers to move away from ills rather than toward goals. Moving sideways, out of trouble, is unsatisfactory. No matter how difficult it is, we must learn to manage complexity and change. Even to an optimist, it is clear that this is difficult. The key is our self-interest. Either we will become better workers and leaders, or we will be finished.

Most of us would be happiest with quick solutions. A manager calls to say: "I have an interview next Tuesday. Could you give me something to read, a list of ideas on interviewing I can use? I can go over it on the plane." Another person wants to better manage his in-basket. It is a mess. His function has grown, and he's been in trouble with his director for being unaware of deadlines on queries assigned to him. A group of women professionals ask how long they must be patient with apathetic managers. In each case the individuals would be happiest if I had an answer which would be immediately effective. The interviewee had to sharpen his resume and practice answering questions about his experience. The real issue is his dawning realization that he needs to learn how to tell his story and to improve his skills in presentation. The manager with the in-basket problem does not yet understand that he must discipline himself to take care of activities that fail to excite him. But he has learned how to sort out and identify his priorities. The women, in a training support group, are beginning to move from dependency and passivity toward autonomy and action. All this takes time. Most of the ideas in this book take time, discipline, and effort.

The great danger for managers rising in the hierarchy is to become separated from accurate information. In the busyness of the day, activities cause increasing isolation and can result in judgments that are ill-advised. Although we recognize this problem, most of us err in focusing on specific activities rather than in gaining perspective and touring the work place to gather data.

Filters further complicate communication. Your perception colors the way you perceive rumors and gossip, how you evaluate programs and people. The perceptions of your listeners color the way you are understood. Rational faith is the basis for decision—not rational judgment.

It is difficult to make sense of, much less to act on, all of the messages, details, demands of superiors and subordinates. If you would be a leader, you must resist the reactive role that is the easier path. Those who succumb to fire fighting and crisis management will seldom enjoy the pleasures of achievement. Some do find excitement in the frenzy of last-minute reports and actions that stave off disasters. You know that you are managing when you move around the system despite the red tape and when you find opportunity in routine assignments. The true test is when you concentrate on that which really matters to the organization and to you.

Your task is to combine effective management behavior with accepted and tested societal values and appropriate goals. That is not easy to do. What are the hidden agendas? How can you find out what is of primary importance to the organization and to you? Sometimes people within the organization do not know what is important. Sometimes even the people in charge do not know what matters. Sometimes they change their minds. They say one thing and mean another. This confuses people and leads to the credibility and morale problems that have beset the FBI and the CIA in the last ten years.

A few years ago, a college that had championed nonelitist education found itself all at once fighting faculty, community groups, students, and staff. Their literature told of the founder's advocacy of education to enable the working class, "the children of shopkeepers and laborers," to earn a living. The continuing education enrollment rose as more working adults returned to school. Despite limited financial resources and classrooms in converted office and factory space, enthusiasm was high. People interested in reviving the city, learning, and teaching had found a place to share ideas. No wonder that the developer of an innovative community education program was puzzled when his ideas were turned down. Plans to promote research of vocational education were rejected. The school cut programs in public health and early childhood education. This lack of support baffled many people. What had happened was that, as the city changed, the land that the college owned rose in value. Soon more people managed property than planned educational policy and programs. They were in the real estate business rather than the education business, but no one noticed. Harassed by the grumblings and protests of activists, the top executives seemed unaware of what was going on. Lacking direction, the institution's excellence declined.

Our daily experience confirms management studies on the unrelenting and capricious nature of work. When you have no time for planning, you face a dilemma. Planning is your heaviest responsibility. It involves the ability to conceptualize and carry out complex ideas, integrate resources, opportunity, and mission. Failures in planning lead to failures in productivity. You are judged on your ability to plan.

The job never ends. You can only, finally, abandon projects. There are too many activities and they change constantly. It is as if life were a kaleidoscope. With the slightest movement a new pattern emerges. There is much guessing and reacting, and few gauges of success. There are seldom desirable standards of performance, and loose ends are ubiquitous. You can never say "everything is finished."

Although specializing in brevity and fragmentation, you must not let the variety distract you from the major themes of the work or from the need to demonstrate understanding of goals and resources. Throughout strong organizations, an important theme runs like a thread. At its best, this theme touches on an admired value, something that people want and believe in. One organization may stress improved productivity. Another organization teams quality with cost reduction. In another, customer service is paramount. Holding to a principle of lean management in a simple structure has enabled more than one major corporation to beat competitors on costs.

More and more, however, corporations give out mixed messages. Although some chief executives preach pioneering, new products may rate little time and garner few rewards. Talk about innovation is unconvincing when the accountants are in control and are only giving out prizes for cost-cutting. It is not so much what you say that counts. What matters is what you do and what you have the people who work with you do. Suspicion and selectivity have their roles. Rumors from reliable grapevines are often the working rubrics of the organization. We question testimonials and exhortations. A colleague remarked to me, partly in truth, that we always pay attention to and remember rumors. At the same time, we are reluctant to accept the official messages and have a hard time learning rules. "Perhaps," he said, "we should teach rules by calling them rumors." To persuade others of what is important means that you have to accept and work with their resistance to your ideas. In turn, your judgment of their messages is tempered by what you have observed or experienced. You need to remain aware of this challenge.

It is confusing when management says one thing and means another. Confusion can also result when listeners do not listen or when they hear the message incorrectly. Recently, the chairman of a multimillion dollar company fired the president who had, in two years, moved the company forward, raised morale, and increased profits. He had an impressive record. Almost everyone was stunned, except for one senior executive who remarked that the president had forgotten that "this is the chairman's popcorn stand." The chairman wanted a high standard of creativity that

was profitable; his president aimed for profit in a creative industry. The president failed to follow the chairman's vision. He had
not asked, "What do you get fired for around here?" He did not
keep his eye on the main event: "Make your boss look good." He
had assumed that the goal was profit. His naivete was his down-
fall. In outstanding organizations, words and action are congru-
ent. They say what they do. They do what they say. They keep it
simple. They have one theme and stick to it.

Despite all of our talk about "the bottom line," if you are wise,
you will never assume that profit is the prime mover. Profit is
necessary, positive cash flow is a happiness, and high morale is
vital. That never means that those are necessarily the main
events. The paramount priority is what the person in charge
wants. Because power shifts easily and swiftly, you need accurate information on who's in charge. Success depends on your
identifying with that person or those people's vision—with the
mission of the organization. If you head a division or office, you
need a subtheme that is aligned with the main theme of the
organization.

If you are the chief executive officer, you need to clarify your
definition of the organization's theme. Can you picture your idea
in detail? Can you make a one-sentence statement of what is
important? Can those who work for you identify with that
theme? How do you know?

The top executive of a steel company announced at a sales
meeting in the early 1960s that the company was no longer in the
steel business but in the business of making money. Some failed
to hear what he was saying, but most were merely confused.
They knew how to sell steel. They obviously could not sell
money. They were to continue selling steel. What did it mean?
What were they to do? The message gave them no clues. There
was nothing at the center. Money-making as a single goal is just
not absorbing to most people.

Perhaps it is too abstract, too difficult to grasp. Although
profits peaked, clerical support was cut. The company imposed
directives on the managers to buy American cars instead of for-
eign ones. The rules on expense accounts were tightened. The
executive accurately foresaw hard times coming, but he lacked

the vision to identify a mission that the employees could understand. As confusion mounted about what they were doing and
where they were going, people literally began to fall apart. Alco-
holism rose. One top manager slashed his wrists, another found
himself screaming on the subway, four or five went to various
clinics where they were prescribed tranquilizers. Over coffee, the
salesmen would compare symptoms. Anticipating decline and a
smaller pie to share, some began to cut in on other people's accounts. Today the company is barely in either the steel or the
money business.

Despite our romantic notions of people pulling together and
doing their best in adversity, the reverse can happen. Sometimes
people panic. Panic is not pretty. Even when it is not ugly, panic
can result in mindless, even stupid, behavior. Fortunately, such
action can be stopped. Drawing upon common values, people
can work toward mutual goals. Our culture provides blueprints
and tools that we ignore at our peril (see Figure 1).

An examination of American values may help chief executives,
future leaders, and managers assume an integrated and thoughtful approach to getting the work done. What does your work
place stand for? What do we want to stand for? For more than 350
years in America, certain ideas based on an ethos of good sense,
good will, and good character have endured. These relatively
unchanging values exist in our minds, but we seldom think about
them. They have been generalized from our history and experience. Examined, they can provide us with insights into the main
event and the values of our organization.

The idea of the worth of the individual is one such value. Every
person, we believe, possesses dignity and is worthy of concern.
Each of us is entitled to freedom, privacy, comfort, property,
health, autonomy, and civil and friendly treatment. We want to
have influence over others, to be recognized as individuals, and
to be successful. We'd like to see ourselves and others as golden,
and to be treated as golden.

Success is linked with the extraordinary. Our ideal is the
self-made person rising from rags to riches. To get there, you can
build a reputation for unique products and services. Your work,

your organization, can be distinguished by quality. High standards and high expectations are elements of winning.

Worth of the individual
Honesty
Simplicity
Cooperation and honest competition
Courage and adventure
Discipline
Order and thrift
Responsibility
Humility
Innovation
Winning and achieving results
Optimism
Rational and reasonable behavior
Success
Upward mobility
Status and the good life
Comfort
Equal rights and equal opportunity
Freedom
Citizenship
Popularity
Privacy
Friendliness
Humor

Figure 1.   Values and themes.

A country store opened last year in my city. It is enjoyed by many. The meats are first-rate, cut to order, and the store stocks an increasing array of high quality goods. What makes the marketplace outstanding is that the owners have found their theme. They know that courtesy is never out-of-date. They unfailingly say "hello" to each person who comes in the store. They know their customers by name and say "thank you" with equal warmth to those who buy a half-pound of hamburger as those who order ten pounds of filet mignon. At the end of a long work day, I find my spirits revived by their attention. Their winning humor and friendliness add to the warmth and draw in the customers.

We want our winners to exhibit traits of cooperation, honest competition, self-discipline, courage, and humility. We see responsibility as a key virtue. One former high government official told me that upon taking office, he sat at his desk and set down his own rules of behavior. He wrote that he would say "no" to any action that he would not want to see in the Washington *Post* or recorded in the National Archives. He knew more sophisticated decision making tools but found none faster or more effective. His job required instant response to a dizzying number of special cases. He had to perceive and react without hesitation to swiftly changing public sentiment. He proved to himself that, in the long run, it was easiest to be responsible and to tell the truth. When he left office, he never worried about how his work would be judged. His deliberate commitment to a standard of behavior, he believed, enabled him to survive in a difficult job.

Organizations benefit when they require that managers always consider honesty an alternative. Sometimes the whole truth is inappropriate. You must distinguish between truth-telling and telling everything. It is hard to know what the truth is. Even should you know, tell little. If you tell everything, no one will trust you with secrets. You have to assess your situation and act with discretion, not candor. You can refuse to lie. It is easier; you have less to remember and to keep straight. We do enjoy stories of those who tell tall tales and skirt the truth, but we require exoneration through a standard of integrity and generosity. Honor and winning go together.

We love to win, to hit home runs. We love those who hit home runs. We enjoy the fruits of our optimism and labor—achieving goals and seeing results. Winning comes in different forms. Some achieve popularity, others autonomy, recognition, and fame. Some look for wealth and others peace of mind. Advancement and prestige are the rewards for some while others seek opportunities to serve. We feel guilty or ambivalent about wealth and power perhaps because we prize innocence. Money and power seem sinful. We like to be seen as striving to achieve goals through our personal and honest efforts. No obstacle is ever too big for determined action. In our novels, theater, and film, we admire portrayals of those who grow and achieve through unflinching optimism and incredible effort. We applaud, in particular, the underdog who comes up a winner, whether it be an organization or an individual. The films *Rocky, Breaking Away,* and *Grapes of Wrath* show us in Steinbeck's words, "the people who survive." Honest labor comes in many varieties. I like the television commercial where John Houseman, identified in our minds as the ultimate high- and tough-minded law professor of *Paper Chase,* tells us that a brokerage house "makes money the old-fashioned way—through hard work."

Although securing material comforts gratifies us and for some becomes an obsession, many appreciate the ideals of our Puritan and pioneer forbears. We recognize that conspicuous consumption demonstrates a lack of social conscience. The hedonism of these times can never obscure our respect for honesty and simplicity. Hard work, orderliness, and thrift remind us of good old days that may never have been. It is no matter. Ben Franklin stood for themes that still ring true.

Americans support rational approaches. Having faith in human reason, we look upon clarity and order as virtues. We manipulate our environment to emphasize practical rather than theoretical knowledge. Our watchwords are "workable solutions and pragmatic applications." Suspicious of theory, we may decide too quickly that our definition of order is best and that we know what is rational. We like the scientific method but are somewhat ambivalent about science and technology. In the last few years, however, our anxiety about Dr. No and other mad scientists with their monstrous hardware has given way to acceptance and affection for R2D2 of *Star Wars* and for a technology that is often a toy in our own hands.

We look for easy, quick solutions. Often that is appropriate, but sometimes we may have to act with patience. Complex and sensitive problems may require complex and sensitive actions as well as patience. A crisis has a life span of its own which is not always within our control. However, if you propose restraint as part of your main theme, you can create new problems for yourself. We are an impatient people. We admire restraint but identify more easily with those who take swift action. You may need to hook your requirement for patience to more popular and accepted values such as cooperation or optimism and effort.

In business, the truism goes: "That which counts is that which can be counted." We aim to be first. We like to be recognized as authorities. Many individuals and many organizations—banks, high technology companies, pharmaceuticals, and food processors—find their main events in a reputation for being first in solid up-to-date research. You can exhort people to be first, to improve sales by 30%, to increase profit by a million dollars. Realistic and measurable goals enable you to see productivity and show others what you have accomplished. This needn't mean, however, that meaning lies in measurement. Measurable goals, deadlines, and tangible products count. There is, however, another dimension. As the poet e.e. cummings put it "everything that is measurable is not art everything that is not art is untrue and everything that is untrue is not worth a good god damn." The true value of our efforts may lie in our achievement of a standard of excellence. Our main event may be the spirit and health of a hopeful enterprise, or the genuine good humor and smiles of a happy client, employee, employer, or colleague. Top managers communicate values that go beyond profits. For many, there is a pleasure, not measurable, when a paycheck merely frees you to do what you love.

For all of us, the paycheck should allow a reasonable standard of personal comfort. You want to improve your appearance and comfort, to save money, to collect the possessions that you enjoy. You want to enjoy beautiful objects and the pleasures of the good life. These have been American goals since the early settlers brought English goods with them to Plymouth or St. Mary's City, and carried Connecticut brass clocks on the covered wagons across country. To live better is part of our lives, not just our dreams. We see no shame in profit if it lies within a framework of honest labor and generosity. Alexis de Tocqueville noted, as an outsider in the eighteenth century, that we hold to equal rights in social and political matters and equality of opportunity in economic affairs. This distinction serves the free-enterprise system.

We resent inappropriate authoritarian relationships. Our thinking reflects a deep aversion to coercive restraints. Confident of our competence in making decisions, and in our reasonableness, we want to manage our own affairs. We relinquish freedom uneasily. We prefer to talk about rights rather than duties. Aspirations of upward mobility, status, and equality for us and for others are prime movers. Because we demand freedom of choice ourselves, we must, when we think about it, respect the rights of others and can appreciate how others resent authoritarian behavior.

Today we face dynamic, constant change. Just to catch your breath can be a job. Keeping an eye on old, tested, and trusted values provides you with what Alvin Tofler called "stability zones." These are "certain enduring relationships that are maintained despite all kinds of other changes." Some examples are a cherished car, afternoons spent sailing, close friends, family, a comfortable style of dress, enduring habit patterns, and tested values. You can never suppress change; you can only try to manage it. With your preferred values as a conscious "stability zone," you can forecast what you might or should do in the future. You can inventory your strengths to determine:

What you are doing.

What you can do.

What you should do.

What you might do.

Your sense of self-worth, social responsibility, and value strengthens you and enables you to overcome internal and external blocks.

Your organization cannot stand for all of these values, but a single-minded focus on a value is a sign of a well-managed organization, and can become the symbol of the place. Thomas Peters of McKinsey reports that new product themes dominate 3M and Hewlett Packard, that IBM employees all talk of solving customer problems, that the Dana Corporation stresses cost reduction and productivity improvement. Some themes, of course, combine several major values. Peters states, however, that an outstanding organization, aware that too many messages cause confusion, "has one theme and sticks to it." At a major airline, the chairman's daily staff meeting centers on a simple control system reporting the previous day's on-time statistics. This enables the airline to put emphasis on the challenge of customer relations. Immersion in that particular detail does not destroy delegation nor interfere with competent supervision. It enables the chairman and his top executives to know what is going on. When you know what you stand for and declare that message, you can act. Clarification of what is important makes it easier for you to move forward.

Like "A–OK," "Project Management" is a term of the space age. As an organizational main event, it an old idea. Project managers built Ebla, engineered the Great Pyramids of Giza, constructed Machu Picchu and the Great Wall of China. Others orchestrated the festivals of Dionysus in Athens, put on the circuses in Rome, and worked on the Cathedral at Chartres. Marco Polo was one, as was Christopher Columbus, Thomas Burbage, George Washington Carver, Wolfgang Amadeus Mozart, and Helen Hull. Each had a vision. They often achieved ends different from what they planned, and may have never understood or seen the historical significance of their acts. They provide examples of excellence and achievement. History reveals tantalizingly little of how they conceived and clarified their great ideas, how they planned and carried out the work, and how they enlisted others in the enterprise.

Our health and self-esteem rest on worthwhile work. Interference with such common sense leads to frustration, neurosis, dullness, and other ills. We can achieve relief only by action toward autonomy. With all the unfinished business around, with all the work in the world that remains to be done, it is astounding that we fail to put our energy to work on the needs of adults to involve themselves in a responsible way with work that matters. Job enrichment can be a useful tool, but jobs needn't always be enriched. They do need to be connected to the organizational main events.

We know that quality of craftsmanship and productivity are problems, but few managers communicate the importance of these issues. Look to organizations where quality and productivity are valued and see what messages management communicates. A woman working on the assembly line at the Steinway plant in Long Island City was asked what she was doing and responded in a surprised way, "Why I build fine pianos, of course."

When the theme of your organization is clear, your managers can see how to fit in their projects. Priorities, delegation, and methods fall into place. International Business Machines, with its emphasis on customer service, keeps the theme in mind even in its college recruiting program. Four interviewers and a supervisor may arrive on a campus for two days. They may see more than two hundred students. Perhaps two will be hired. That seemed cost-ineffective to me until the supervisor said, "I come along to be sure that everything we do reinforces one main idea. Each of these students is a potential customer. Someday when they buy computers, we want them to think IBM." Their attention contrasted sharply to a leading New York bank who treated interviewees so cavalierly that several told me that they would never open an account in that bank.

It is crucial for an organization to have a strong positive image. You need to take the time to develop a positive mental model of the ideas, people, and environment of your organization. You have a vision of the direction that you want your organization to take, or that you want your life to take. This picture may be blurred. If your thinking is out of focus, writing your ideas down may make them clearer, may force you to be more exact. The more vivid your ideas, the more likely that you will be able to translate them into action.

Creating and maintaining a positive picture will provide hope to those who work with you. People need to be encouraged and to believe that achievement is anticipated. Clarify the values and the projects that make your ideas concrete and empathize with people's desire to behave responsibly. You can build your plan on the assumption that others will shoulder burdens and fight for the right.

If you are in charge of your organization, develop your thinking of *what* your enterprise is about, *how* you plan to carry out your plans, *who* the players are, *where* and *when* this will take place. Double-check by assessing your risks. Ask yourself *why* and consider whether your plan fills a real need—a need that the chief executive officer, the directors, and your customers can see (see Figure 2). Your plan needn't be long. A page may be enough, but it should address directly what you believe is important.

What do we do?

Does our work fill a recognizable need?

How do we know?

Who else sees this need?

What are the alternatives?

How do we know that our way is best?

Figure 2. Questions for planning.

If you run a subsystem, you need to examine your understanding of the organization's theme. Read everything—annual reports, newsclippings, long-range plans, the chief executive officer's speeches—but look harder at what is going on. Interview people. If possible, talk with your chief executive officer. Check with people in as many divisions as possible: marketing, production, personnel, finance, legal. This exercise will serve several purposes:

You will gather important data.

You will practice "touring" the organization which, in time, could be an invaluable management tool.

You can gain allies to help you do your job.

You'll probably gather conflicting information and face a challenge in defining your organization's theme. Clarify your thoughts and write a brief, detailed plan of your division's work which remains consistent with the organization's theme and values. (see Figure 3). Consider your risks. Include a simple control system that is based on the organization's theme.

As John Dewey taught us, we learn from what we do, and most of us experience only bureaucratic carefulness. That will do no longer. More than profit and productivity is at stake. Clarifying our own values and conceptions of the organization's mission helps us maintain a psychologically healthy position. Working toward values that we respect and with which others identify moves us and our organization toward mental health.

THEME _____

_____

_____

_____

PLAN OR PROJECTS THAT SUPPORT THEME

_____

_____

_____

_____

_____

CHECKLIST
Structure
Resources
Timing
Strategies
Risks
Alternatives
Communication plan

Figure 3.   The main event planning work sheet.

Two

Chaos Will Stop at Three O'Clock

SETTING PRIORITIES

Ironed sheets are a health hazard.
ERMA BOMBECK

Everything worth doing is not necessarily worth doing well.
KINGMAN BREWSTER

Many non–main events masquerade as main events because they fill the day. If unchecked, they take over. To counter this, you must not only identify your main events, but also distinguish between necessary activities and clutter. The clutter must be discarded, for unchecked, it is a cancer that can kill. If your days are a series of meetings interrupted by irrational demands from your boss, you may complain that it is impossible to worry about main events. The in-basket overflows, fifteen pink slips of paper mutely badger you to return telephone calls, and your monthly report is overdue. You have no time to think—to figure out what you should be doing. It is no comfort to know that managers everywhere dash from task to task throughout the day, all participants in some mad tea party.

Some years ago, I worked for a vice-president who later moved on to another organization. I inherited his position. My first day on the job, I discovered that he had left me a list of suggestions. It ended with an admonition to make an appointment with myself every Friday afternoon at 2:15 to look ahead to the next week. I was told to study, add, and alter priorities and to kill off projects that I could no longer afford. The note ended: **FAILURE TO DO THIS WILL BE AT YOUR PERIL**. He was right.

Look to your own priorities. Consider your organization's mission and responsibilities. From your brief analysis of your organization, its values, or those values you wish to see incorporated, consider what you can do to turn those concepts into reality (see Figure 4). You might compare your company's annual report with that of your major competitor. How do the messages differ? What is the financial picture of each? How are your missions similar? How are they different? How are each of you looking forward? How do you fit in? Trade magazines, newsletters, and local press articles can help you see where you, your industry, your organization, or your division are headed.

Important main events should be obvious when you consider how your job relates to the major theme or mission of the organization. Your job description should reflect this relationship. If you don't have a position description that accurately describes what you do, write one. Many managers tell me that their position description bears no resemblance to their work. They are waiting for someone else to fix it. No one else will. Writing one is worth the effort, whether you are president of the company or the manager of sales or procurement. This enables you to clarify what you do that is important and how it is related to the major theme and mission. It may not be necessary for your position description to be in your official personnel file, but your supervisor should agree with its content. This document could be useful in a merger or at appraisal time if it accurately describes your responsibilities.

What would the chief executive officer think I do that matters?

What are my major projects and how do they relate to the organization's theme and mission?

What activities would I be wise to delegate or train someone else to do?

What "clutter" should I eliminate?

What action should I take to tie myself more closely to the organization's major theme and mission?

Figure 4.   Relationship of position to organizational theme and mission.

In doing this, give special thoughts to what you should be doing: developing new customers, producing a quality product, developing cost-saving procedures, turning an idea into an organization. You may realize that you fail to spend enough time on these prime topics. Whatever gets in your way is a non–main event. Some of these are activities that require someone's attention: time keeping, personnel actions, responding to employee complaints, reporting on activities, requisitions, answering queries from the media, from customers, clients, and constituents. If you attend to activities that others should take care of— this is clutter.

Events that are neither main events nor necessary activities are also clutter. What is clutter? Clutter is that which doesn't count, that which detracts from your ability to progress. Clutter is often a blot that prevents you from seeing what matters. You may fail to see that old priorities are no longer valuable. If you do not give attention to clutter, you will find yourself shooting off arrows at an increasing rate with no discernible target. If you cut clutter, you will increase your likelihood of survival. You will also have an opportunity to improve productivity and do what is important.

Oftentimes, favored activities prove to be clutter because they simply do not move the organization forward. People do things that they find interesting. Managers are fascinated to see how many ways subordinates avoid doing what they don't like to do. As is said, "People will only do what they damn well please." We all trap ourselves this way. Many people bring inappropriate tasks with them when they move into management. They want to continue being salespersons or technical or professional specialists. This leaves too little time for the risky and difficult parts of the job—for often tedious but necessary action.

Open and searching examination of your job and its tasks provides insights and can help you deal with the misconceptions that operate at work. There is an archaic canon by which many managers still live. The results of adherence to this canon remind us that there is a lot of fantasy in organizations which masquerades as tough-mindedness. These notions include the following:

Passive acceptance is preferred from employees
   Be reasonable; do it my way.

Discovering knowledge is for bosses
   If it were a good idea, I would have had it.

The voice of authority is to be obeyed
   I know what is best; be obedient.

Ideas of subordinates are inconsequential
   Trust me, my ideas are better.

Feelings are irrelevant at work
   I am cool and logical in all my actions.

Bosses know the best way to get things done
   I am the authority.
Instant answers are important
   I have all the answers.

These misconceptions create incalculable clutter and prevent us from managing effectively. There are those who say that a culture must hold some people back to allow others to succeed. I am not one of them. Executive triage is unnecessary. In most management situations, control in the style of a Victorian parent or a Marine sergeant is inappropriate. Conducting a symphony, leading a platoon in battle, taking scouts on an outing, producing a play, directing a space launch, and sailing a sailboat on the Chesapeake may be exceptions. In most situations, those who adhere to such archaic canons must devote considerable energy to surveillance, rule making, and enforcement.

Productivity improvement, profit, customer service, national security, and other main events get less attention than they deserve. So many supervisors behave according to variations of these misconceptions that we keep thousands of labor and employee relations professionals busy. Our calendars are overloaded with unnecessary grievance cases. In time, an organization gets the kind of labor relations that it deserves.

Because most of us are unaware of how we really spend our time, much of the clutter in our life is invisible. The first step is discovery through auditing of your time. For ten days, keep a log of your activities and energy levels. Note what you are doing: reviewing reports, delegating tasks, writing, telephoning, attending meetings. See what main events are being addressed. Question your tasks. Question your assumptions. Review your resources: budget, personnel, technology. What procedures can be trimmed or dropped? What forms can be eliminated or simplified? Are you pushing yourself or are you missing opportunities to work on challenging assignments? Are you overmanaging? Most executives do not spend their time the way that they think that they do (see Figure 5). Have your key subordinates keep a similar log. You will immediately see the value of work simplification and time management.

DATE	TASK	NOTES

8 am _____

_____

9 am _____

_____

10 am _____

_____

11 am _____

_____

12 n _____

_____

1 pm _____

_____

2 pm _____

_____

3 pm _____

_____

4 pm _____

_____

5 pm _____

_____

6 pm _____

_____

Figure 5. Daily time log.

Review the different actions that you and your staff take and consider the opportunity and true cost of each. Ask yourself "What is the potential contribution of the activity?" If it is a boring but necessary task, be sure that it is well done and put out of the way. Ask yourself if the right person is doing the job. You will discover that some things should never be done at all. You can find opportunities in obligations. In a meeting, look for new people to meet, gather information assertively, lobby for a cause. At a party, strengthen relationships with colleagues and staff.

A popular management theory often stated by Peter Drucker is that 80% of what we achieve is accomplished in 10−20% of our time. My experience and that of others agree. If true, and we work forty to fifty hours a week, there is profit in dedicating eight to twelve hours, at least, to moving forward on the main events. Many managers have found that by studying their logs and the logs of their subordinates that they can eliminate clutter and inappropriate tasks by 50−75%. This can free up ten to twenty hours more for main events which could increase productivity by the 50% that Drucker and others see as necessary and possible.

Various managers have pointed out behavior that contributes to waste and clutter such as:

Failure to understand time planning.

Inability to distinguish important from unimportant elements.

Underestimation of time and effort.

Too many rules and procedures.

Failure to plan adequately.

Allowing anxiety about time to rob you of energy.

Inability to balance work standards and elements of time.

Failure to find ways to simplify tasks, improve problem solving, delegate tasks, use technology effectively.

Unnecessary reports that no one reads.

Too little task variety.

Lack of control over job.

Too many approvals required.

Other people's misuse of time.

These are difficult problems for all of us. They can only be solved through discipline and effort.

Problems with time management often relate to feelings of powerlessness. Rosabeth Kanter has pointed out that this is especially true when there is little recognition of the unit's work, when there is little contact with top management, and when the focus is within the work unit. If you are trying to improve time management and productivity, an attempt to connect the work with the mission, the main event, is vital. Look for ways to increase the time that you and your staff meet with senior officials, and provide opportunities for subordinates to participate in projects that are important to current problem areas. There may be ways for people to work across organizational lines, on committees, or on task forces. This would add variety to their jobs, enable them to learn about other units and people, and would serve the purpose of increasing your sources of information. If you can eliminate some of the factors that contribute to powerlessness, you may tap new reservoirs of energy.

The question of clutter often gets down to work standards. Not everything that is worth doing is worth doing well. "Gold plating" tasks is the curse of middle management. Secretaries retype reports, specialists reedit them, chartists redraw the charts, the typing is again redone. Often, the product is only for internal consumption. Remember that the demands of customers, clients, and constituents drive organizations. In your work, measure your output in terms of meeting those needs. Someone recently told me that she had monitored one internal report that was retyped thirty-eight times. The last was the result of a secretary who decided to change each *that* to *which*. Ashleigh Brilliant captured this behavior in *Pot Shot 116*, "Before burning these papers, let me make sure they're in alphabetical order." There is poignancy in the statement "I don't want it good; I want it Tuesday." Perfect typing has its place, but it is sometimes unnecessary. This is not to argue for sloppy work but for standards appropriate to the task.

People may gold plate their jobs when they no longer have enough to do. This is where auditing time and redesigning the organization plays an essential part. Many people advance as professionals because they do their work extremely well with great attention to detail. As managers, they fail because they want everything done to match their own image. They rewrite competent studies written by their staff, drive subordinates wild demanding reworking of reports that no one reads, and continually make contradictory changes. It is necessary, if you are serious about productivity, to balance the time and cost of projects with the results.

Robert Townsend has suggested that you can handwrite an answer on an original letter, have it photocopied and mailed out within minutes of receipt. This act is clear, personal, economical, and effective, particularly between people who know one another. Often a telephone call is better than a letter. A stop by the office may be best. You could make it a rule that nothing routine is rewritten. Some managers find that their employees respond to simple but high standards for usage. A sample correspondence book helps too. Save perfectionism for high-priority projects.

Your organization may be so addicted to crisis management and so resistant to planning that you feel you are all alone. Although fire fighting is what makes some people's lives exciting, it is a sign of mediocre management. Managers often put their best people on projects of little value. They assign others to something that may be important to "them." They ask for a report of vague purpose "just in case." Busyness, new tasks piled on old, no time to think or consider the main event can result in clutter and a losing style. Giving up the excitement of crisis management starts with figuring out what you like best about your job. If it is the craziness and frenetic behavior, management is not your game. You should consider being a brilliant loner. Fire fighting style will lead to lowered productivity, and that is bad management. If you would learn to lead, consider the drummer who said, "It's what I don't play that counts. Every note has to be important." This means discipline, careful craftsmanship, and rewarding yourself and others for successful problem solving.

The high-priority jobs are where you should spend your time. Set deadlines to allow for interruptions, errors, illness, poor work days, supply shortages, and other problems in the organization. I figure out how much time a job should take if everything works. Then, depending on the organization, I double or triple my estimate. Know how long it takes your staff to accomplish their

various regular tasks. Find out why. Understand, at least super-
ficially, what is involved in ordering supplies, in using your new
hardware, in arranging travel. Help other people learn how to
make accurate estimates and encourage them to find ways to save
time and effort.

One manager told me that she has disciplined herself to keep
"Necessary Activities" in a single file folder on her desk. She has
but one place to check daily for action items, for forms for the
current month's report. Her secretary abstracts various reports,
press clippings, and departmental memos that he thinks are
important in a one-page sheet of highlights. This enables them
both to stay informed, keeps her from drowning in paper, and
enlists the secretary in the cause of cutting clutter.

When Franklin Roosevelt was president, Raymond Moley, a
member of his original brain trust, had the task of reading dozens
of daily newspapers from all over the country. He would prepare
a one-page précis and then underline in red what was really
important for the President to read. That is really cutting to the
heart of the matter. It also illustrates Theodore Levitt's advice
that "there is only one way to manage anything and that is to
keep it simple." Nowhere does this ring truer than when we ap-
praise the day's events that cause us to say wearily, "everything
takes longer."

In examining ten-day accounts of their time and of their subordinates' time, managers have discovered many ways to cut
clutter. Most of them are obvious methods of protecting time and
energy. Nevertheless, until you make a habit of concentrating on
important activities, you may find yourself drifting back into
wasting time on unimportant or unnecessary trivia (see Figure
6).

People often complain that their superiors burden them with
task upon task and end up smothering them in work. This underscores the importance of learning to accurately estimate the time
certain tasks require. If you know what your main events are,
what tasks are assigned to you, and how much time you need for
each activity, then you have important data. You can ascertain
whether your assignments are realistic. If they are not, you have
some information with which to base a discussion with your

supervisor. You may be able to eliminate tasks of lesser importance or delegate them to others. A meeting of this sort with your superior can help you verify your priorities, and develop ways to avoid distracting clutter.

To create free time in your schedule, find ways to dovetail or streamline activities. Your secretary can handle routine correspondence, maintain your follow-up system, and assign priorities to clerical duties. You may need several in-baskets. One should be for main events including messages from your key staff, your boss, and your family. You will benefit from disciplining yourself to go through the main event basket frequently.

Assign yourself large blocks of time for study, creative effort, and planning. Unless you make the effort, it will not happen.

Keep an appointment with yourself on Friday at 2:15 to plan the week ahead.

Have a plan for each day and take time to arrange your tasks in priority order.

Give time to the main event before the pressing, but less important, immediate problems.

Assign difficult projects to a time when you are most energetic.

Ask yourself if there is an easier way.

Set a rational and regular time for mail, telephone, in-basket, and necessary chores.

Cluster appointments and leave some days unscheduled.

Tour the office often to find out what people are doing.

Carry reading material with you and use waiting time to stay informed.

Reward clutter-cutting when you and others do it.

Figure 6. Keeping on target.

This may mean that you will have to arrange to have your phone calls held or you will have to leave the office to work in the library or some other quiet place. If you want to do something that is important to you, schedule a date. You may postpone it, of course, as events close in. If so, you will know that you have postponed it. That doesn't mean that you should punish yourself, but consider it a warning. You are failing to accomplish something that you want to do.

Getting started is often a major hurdle. Alan Lakein suggests that when all else fails, you can overcome procrastination on an important job by doing nothing—in a structured way. You stare at the task for fifteen minutes. During that time you do not allow yourself to do anything else. You do not daydream or think about any other subject. You just sit and stare at the job. For some reason, guilt maybe, you will find yourself working vigorously before the time is up. Fifteen minutes can seem like a long time when you watch it pass.

When you review your log, see how much time you give to touring the shop. An important reason to cut out trivia is to give yourself more time for this. Touring the shop can be a most productive activity. Although managers who tour know that it is invaluable, few do it. Most sit in their offices, secure in their tight little territory. If you want to increase productivity, walk around and ask employees what they are working on. You may be surprised. You could also ask them what you do that gets in the way of their doing a better job.

Touring the office and taking time each Friday to consider where you are going can have major impact on your productivity. Both are simple to do but require discipline and practice. If you do them regularly, they will become habits.

Both actions can change your thinking about your priorities. In the spirit of developing a healthy fear of system overload, that means killing off pet projects. Projects are not children. Using techniques from strategic planning you can ask yourself:

What am I doing?
What do my logs, my tours of the shop, and various information sources tell me?

What can I do?
There are only 168 hours in a week.
What should I do?
Who else must I satisfy?
What might I do?
Have I considered the options?

After you have crossed out the pet projects that you are killing off, the tasks that you are delegating to others, and the things that do not need doing, you can assign priorities to the activities that are left (see Figure 7).

Date _____

PRIORITY	PROJECT	DUE DATE
_____	_____	_____
_____	_____	_____
_____	_____	_____
_____	_____	_____
_____	_____	_____
_____	_____	_____
_____	_____	_____
_____	_____	_____
_____	_____	_____
_____	_____	_____

Reminder: Objectives are not cast in concrete; they may be changed as new priorities arise.

Figure 7.   Weekly list.

I use a four-star system. The most urgent and vital tasks rate four stars, a rather important, steady project may rate two or three stars, and an old or potentially important new project may rate one. If you use a system like this, set yourself a goal for new stars. Make new product- or service- development high on your list of main events. This is not because newness itself should have high value, but because changing conditions require new solutions. The organization that continues with the tried and true could find itself with a lot of old and fading stars and no four-stars at all.

Make it clear (by your own actions) that you are looking for innovative approaches and actions. "Find it, fix it, try it" have been many leaders' key words for improving productivity and avoiding the slow death that can come with relying smugly on steady projects.

Look at your "old stars" coldly. Maybe you can afford them, but it may be better to eschew sentimentality. If the rewards have paled—psychologically and financially—a clean death may be less painful than a lingering one. You can save your life if you "know when to fold."

It is risky to develop new projects and kill others. That is the manager's job. You need to take swift action but you need, also, to be thoughtful. This is but another paradox of management.

Killing off projects can be difficult. Agnes Allen's maxim is the best one that I know: "It is easier to get into anything than to get out of it." You may have to continue with unprofitable old stars. They then become "necessary non-main events." The lesson that they teach us, especially in hard times, is to allocate future resources with care. Should you get into this new project, acquire this company, start a new service? What is the worst thing that can happen if you do? What is the worst thing that can happen if you do not? Every choice has its cost. There is no such thing as a free ticket. There is both opportunity and cost in each.

Some years ago, I began a new enterprise which was instantly and unexpectedly so busy that in contrast, a department store in December would have seemed tranquil. One day an employee commented that no one knew what anyone else was doing. I looked around and realized that we were all active, but I could not tell what we were accomplishing. I sent everyone a brief memo that read: "Chaos will stop at 3 p.m. on Thursday. We will close the office and meet together to look at our goals, resources, and priorities." The memo itself had a remarkable effect. Smiles and laughter replaced harried expressions. The meeting was successful and started us on a group commitment to create a special service organization. This led us to develop a weekly series of career and professional development meetings which continued over the next three years. Together we eliminated clutter, identified necessary activities and deadlines, and simplified procedures, but most of all we celebrated our own struggle against chaos. We worked together on a number of tasks. Our first step was to look at all of our programs and services. We gauged opportunity and cost and the potential contribution of different activities. We assessed and determined what profit we were after.

Next, we studied each major program and asked the following: "If we were not in this, would we go into it?" If the answer was no, we made plans to get out of it. There were no resources for a lot of things that it would have been nice to do or to have. As Peter Drucker says,

> This calls for painful decisions and risky ones. But that, after all, is what managers are paid for. The hardest part, often, is finding the courage to say "we're not going to make that anymore or we're going to close down that operation or withdraw that service." Such decisions require thoughtful answers to rigorous questions.

These decisions hurt. We look in vain for sources of courage. Our pride is involved. From our childhood we have been admonished "to stick it out." Giving up is embarrassing. We are told that "winners never quit and quitters never win." The bed that we make is the one in which we must lie. These messages make it hard for us to abandon projects that drain our resources. It was only recently that I learned that Gambler's Anonymous is made up mostly of people who didn't know "when to get up and walk away." Every once in a while, we all need a fresh start.

We can reward ourselves as we struggle against clutter and chaos and toward courage. I believe in celebrating when you achieve goals and finish difficult tasks. You can celebrate a successful opening night, procedures that cut paper costs by 20%, a training program that achieves its results, a new product that meets customer needs. This enables you to reinforce improvement. Each month, you could write a report of your accomplishments, including cutting down on non-main events and improving your efficiency in dealing with necessary activities. Look for ways to encourage yourself and others and to reinforce and reward improvement. Let your boss know.

In that 2:15 meeting with yourself on Friday afternoon, take yourself and your work seriously. Test the variables. Maintain a cheerful outlook. Look for positives in negative situations and learn to be watchful for negative elements that could destroy your positive efforts.

You need not do this alone. Talk to others. There are colleagues and those on your staff who will understand some goals better than you. Others will have ideas about how to simplify and to eliminate tasks. Seek out their ideas for improvement. Ask people in other offices for help.

A manager told me of an important lesson he learned in his first supervisory job. He landed a grant for a million dollars. It seemed such an incredible sum that the responsibility awed him. Anticipating a budget system too complex for his own experience, he called the comptroller who, understanding the situation, dropped by to see him bringing two file folders. One was marked **Paid** and the other was **Unpaid**. The comptroller said, "If you keep all vouchers, bills, and purchase orders in either one folder or the other, you'll have no trouble monitoring the project." It was true.

List-making is another activity so simple that you may overlook its effectiveness as a management tool. Years ago, Charles Schwab, an early president of the Bethlehem Steel Company, hired a consultant to help him become more effective. Clutter was crowding out important matters. The consultant told Schwab to make a list of things to do each day and to work on each item until finished. Perhaps Schwab learned from this the pleasure of crossing tasks off lists. This in itself is one of the rewards of clutter-cutting.

Schwab found that this simple method enabled him and his executives to improve their effectiveness. Three months after starting this regimen, he sent the consultant a check for $25,000. This incident proves again that the uncomplicated system is the one that produces results. A simple, flexible plan can enable you to live and work more intelligently. If you keep your list of daily and weekly objectives handy, you can act positively whenever you get muddled. The daily list is your best friend and strongest weapon against clutter.

Three

Bits and Pieces

CONTROLLING YOUR ENVIRONMENT

*If you don't rehearse over and over, you're going to be surprised
in space. And the surprised man, out there, is the dead
one. We get ready, then, by trying to surprise ourselves.*
RAY BRADBURY

*The mind is an enchanted loom where millions of flashing
shuttles weave a dissolving pattern, always a
meaningful pattern though never an abiding one.*
SIR CHARLES SHARRINGTON

As a carrier of your organization's vision, you have an important job in remembering, rehearsing, and helping others to remember the main event. This would be easier to do if there were fewer interruptions. Fragmentation characterizes the day. We illustrate Einstein's law of dynamic bodies constantly affected by other bodies in continuous motion and change. Did life always seem to be made up of tiny bits of time, of particles? In a sixty-second period, if you pay attention to four discrete actions while unnumbered thoughts pass through your mind, your attention becomes shattered. It is a triumph when you find an uninterrupted hour for a major project. Time hurries us as it does in a French farce. I often feel like I am on a cart pulled by runaway horses. It was Bertrand Russell who first noted that life is like a film. This simile is a by-product of our technology. We wonder how many frames there are to a second.

The challenge is to maintain control over the main event, and the fragments, as you are interrupted and as you interrupt others. It seems impossible. The busyness distracts you from stepping back, checking that you are achieving your objectives, and keeping in touch with your self-interest and personal themes. You switch from task to task in no time at all. Everyday, new issues, concerns, and activities demand your attention.

Technology fragments the day. At a rate we could not have imagined even twenty years ago, visitors jet in to see us with little notice and we may jet off to see them. The telephone brings us demands and questions from down the hall, across the country, or across the ocean. The products of copying machines fill the in-basket. The computer assigns work for you to do and issues a reminder two weeks later. The buzz from a gadget on your belt sends you in search of a telephone. The alarm on your watch signals that you are expected somewhere else. Much of this would never have occurred if it had not been for the technology of the second-half of this century. Ten years ago, Father John Culkin, lecturing at Fordham University, said, "A lot has happened lately and most of it plugs into walls." Now, almost everything new operates off silicon chips. Neither electric plugs nor micro-circuits will go away. You can, however, use and control the fragments that they and your work produce, rather than letting them use and control you. It is difficult.

The changes in our world shape our tools, our work environment, and us. We, in turn, shape our tools, our work place, and ourselves. We seldom understand or even notice the socializing influence of organizations. We do no see our own metamorphoses because we take our changing environment for granted. We cannot see it because we are part of it. As Marshall McLuhan said, "Whoever it was who discovered water, you can be sure it was not a fish." But discover the water is what you must do. The skills that can help you are observation and concentration. Although you can be driven by fragmentation, you can also use fragmentation to enhance these skills. This enables you to focus both on what is current and tangible and on that which is long-range and abstract.

Daily, we hear others, and perhaps ourselves, speak of "turning off," "turning on," "tuning in," "pushing the right button." The words refer to our behavior. There is no time to waste. If someone needs to talk with you, you may say "All right, walk with me to my next meeting." You move then from A through B to C without stopping. At A you may be gathering information on two or three different projects, at B you are asked for advice on another problem, and at C you may be speaking on yet another subject as spokesperson for the organization.

It is usually implied that the work controls the manager, nonetheless, you control your work in subtle ways. Managers and social scientists have noticed and identified many parts—roles— that managers play and the importance of role playing. If you study your position description and look at your log, it may be that you find yourself playing a constellation of roles: liaison, trouble shooter, diplomat, organizer, entrepreneur, writer, dispute settler. You can turn your activities to your advantage and use them to implement change. You can select your commitments. Your task is to set your stamp on your unit and set its course. Your ability to move swiftly from role to role enables you to have confidence that the work will be done (see Figure 8).

In the course of a week, you may play ten or twelve roles using innumerable skills. If you assess your own ability to perform these different roles and work to improve the skills that you need, you will be able to achieve the fast takeoff that the times require. Not everyone, of course, can be an expert at everything. Aptitude has its part. Abraham Zaleznik suggests that the strong manager is seldom a strong leader. But you may have to move with moderate success between these two major roles. The manager's role stresses stability, organizing, and controlling activities. Although managerial persistence, tough mindedness, intelligence, and hard work should be effective, sometimes they prove inade-

Forecaster
Monitor
Resource manager
Planner
Figurehead
Communicator
Leader
Spokesperson
Negotiator
Liaison
Trouble shooter
Entrepreneur
Housekeeper
Survivor
Evaluator
Specialist
Coach
Salesperson
Observer
Expert
Listener
Mediator
Mentor

Figure 8. Roles.

quate. Tolerance and good will do not solve all of your problems either. The strong manager needs to be able to move with moderate success to the role of leader. When managerial tinkering proves inadequate, you may be forced to put emphasis on the leader's roles and on developing fresh approaches and choices that will give substance to your vision.

We have all seen how often those elected, appointed, and promoted to high positions fail to mobilize their troops. The problem is not that there is a shortage of good ideas. We have an abundance of answers. Our minds work at least twice as fast as our tongues. The task is to turn those ideas into action. Many people have been unable to move from conceptualizer to information gatherer and disseminator, encourager, negotiator, work evaluator, spokesperson. It takes hard work to learn to move quickly and easily through these roles.

There are six basic purposes of these roles as they relate to your work:

To ensure effective work production.

To design and maintain the stability of the organization.

To adapt to a changing environment.

To ensure that the work is serving the organization's mission.

To serve as a key information link between yourself, the organization, and external organizations.

To operate your own personal work system.

To implement your work, you must look beyond the immediate projects and your personal concerns. You observe, receive, and transmit information. You must be a detective, checking to find out what needs to be done. It becomes necessary for you to interrupt yourself and others, command one program to stop and another to start. As monitor, you check for errors, reward success, and keep alert for shabbiness. Analyzing the situation, you allocate and assign people to their tasks, schedule sequences, and put parts together to form a meaningful whole. Because the organization's stability and growth is no one else's responsibility but yours, you must aim to be a winner and survivor. To do this, you need to retain the ability to confront reality and search for new and better ways to deal with situations. Increasingly, you must make effective use of limited resources and find the strength to persevere. The ability "to hang in," to demonstrate patience and willingness to try new approaches, is necessary for survival. You need the heart of a long-distance runner. This is increasingly difficult when the only certainty is uncertainty. We have to learn when and what to keep and throw away, whom to trust, and how to relax when the ambiguity is overwhelming. This sounds impossible, yet enhancing skills of observation and concentration can help you do this more effectively even if you do not know where you are going, or how and if you will get there.

Your work bears some resemblance to a tree. You need to maintain a vision of upward growth with the trunk as your idea—the main event, the principle action. The branches are elements of the idea. The leaves, flowers, and fruits are the presentations. In managing your work, you must continuously plan, review, and test your theme and mission and secure your goals through combinations of secondary and complementary actions.

If you make a conscious effort to notice everything out of the ordinary, you will improve your memory and become more sensitive to sincerity and insincerity. As you consciously observe other people and are sensitive to what they say and what they do, you will improve your ability to listen and attend effectively. This facilitates your adjustment to whatever may be required and makes it less likely that you will be thrown off guard. More important, as you become more observant, you will be able to appreciate differing personalities and values. This widens your response and enables you to develop a wider repertoire of ways to act in unfamiliar circumstances. You could spend one hour today observing everyone and everything. Then, tomorrow, spend an hour recalling in detail what you observed. Notice how people behave, exactly what they say, how they deal with stress and the fragments of their day. One manager who did this was astounded to find that he had never noticed how often people scratch themselves. This realization made him aware that he was missing other cues. He realized that he failed to pay attention to most people at work and was so busy talking that he never listened.

In particular, notice and copy effective behavior. Most of us do this unconsciously. We pick up styles and way of acting and talking from others: parents, favorite aunts and uncles, teachers, respected bosses, colleagues, and subordinates. More than one generation has learned elegance from Fred Astaire and from Katharine Hepburn. This is not to argue for slavish copying but for learning to act in ways that work. If from your observation, you add behavior that enhances your actions, you will be able to deal more effectively with difficult situations. Innovation is the key. Innovation is the result of hard work and is stimulated by constant keen observation. Most of us believe that we see everything, but often we assimilate nothing. Observation allows us to ascertain how the theme—the main event—perseveres or not, despite obstacles.

Concentration is the quality that allows you to direct all of your forces toward a goal for as long a time as necessary. You can find this quality within yourself and develop it by hard work. The object of your concentration is a concept, your idea of how your organization will flourish and how your contribution will enhance that flourishing. Often, you imagine the products that you would like to produce, the style that would demonstrate your productivity. This requires you to concentrate on abstractions. For this, you need to look into yourself for ideas and feelings not yet developed.

You can practice concentration in meetings with individuals and groups. Observe people's mannerisms, their speech, and their patterns of observation and concentration. Even boring obligatory meetings can be training grounds in observation and concentration.

In a meeting with an employee, for example, allow no distractions. Maintain eye contact, and only look away, and that with circumspection, when you are speaking. Work to observe and notice anything unusual in the other's behavior. The electronic image is useful here. You "tune in" to the other and "turn on" your powers of observation, concentrating on the other's concerns. When the interview is over you "turn off."

You may find, when you practice observing and concentrating on the feelings of yourself and of others, that your education and experience have discouraged interest in and understanding of feelings. It may be necessary to develop a memory of feelings, of imagination. Some people find that wide reading outside of their field opens them to developing this sensitivity. History, novels, plays, biography, and poetry can stimulate the process, as can listening to music, or enjoying painting and sculpture. The feelings are there.

If you repress your feelings, they simply change shape and come out in another form. You may be unpleasantly surprised by your own behavior. You can experience rejection from one person and convert this unconsciously into irritation at someone else. Your anger may be deflected inward and cause you to be depressed or to develop a miserable headache. It is essential that you be aware of, in touch with your feelings. If you are not, you may not be in control of your actions. Another possibility is that you will suppress your feelings and create new emotions to get in your way.

Watch yourself cheerfully and go through life as a detective. Observing yourself and others at work, in the street, on the commuter train, on television, and at play can enlarge this capacity. This provides a store for the future.

It is your job to make good use of everything and every new experience to watch how different people behave in different situations. From this you can collect ideas from everything that you see, read, hear, and feel. This enables you to select what you want to keep. You can discard whatever seems useless. If this is new behavior, you will want to practice in small ways in fairly safe situations. You could ask for feedback and work to improve your skills. There are, in your life as manager, certain high-tension moments on which your survival or the survival of the unit and even the organization may depend. The culmination of a project, a presentation, a paper, a negotiation, or a public event may be such high-tension moments. This requires absolute concentration and accurate observation. Your skills are directed toward those times. This calls for all of your talents, experience, and energy.

With all of the roles that you must play and all of the projects under your control, it is difficult to keep everything in mind at once. There is, indeed, research indicating that people's brains can consciously track or channel approximately seven different ideas at one time. Most of us have many more than seven major responsibilities. No wonder so much goes wrong. The daily list is one life line. Some managers program their projects on a computer and rely on daily or weekly reports to keep them in touch with progress. A manual system is a "Main Event Book." In a large loose leaf notebook you can keep notes and use dividers to separate each project. You can quickly tell where you are on each project, to whom you have delegated action, and what your next move may be. For a single project, you might have important memoranda and materials from pertinent presentations.

The Main Event Book can contain your strategic planning notes and charts, copies of milestone charts, and deadlines. You might want to include communication strategies and assignment of tasks. Wisdom calls for an analysis of dangers and possible areas for errors and optional plans.

The Main Event Book is an inventory of active projects. You can add new ones, see others to conclusion, change directions of some and move others to storage. Some projects in your active inventory may be delayed while you wait for information. An engineering or funding problem may slow you down. The Main Event Book allows you to juggle a large number of projects as you plan steps around setbacks and delays. Some projects can take years to complete and involve thousands of actions by hundreds of people. It has been noted that a highly important managerial skill is the capacity to keep a number of issues in play over a large number of episodes and long periods of time. If you have to be away for a while, this technique cuts catch-up time substantially. You can quickly check through your Main Event Book to see where you are. When you keep a working record of your activities in one place rather than in separate file folders, you can keep your total picture in mind. This enables you to monitor both your time and that of your subordinates. Each morning you can quickly check on each event and make notes for your daily list of what needs to be done, revised, reviewed and communicated.

In some places, a computerized action item records what is to be done, who is responsible and when it is due. A simple manual version (see Figure 9) relates the work assignment to the main event, briefly states *what* is to be done, *who* is to do it, and by *when*, and provides for a response of what has been done. One copy could stay in the Main Event Book. The person to whom action has been delegated should keep the other. This does not prevent everything from going wrong, but I find that it helps. It enables you and your subordinates to know who is doing what and when.

Subject: Due date: Assigned to:

Assignment:

What happened:

Name   Date

Figure 9.   Manual action record.

Employees can be profitably involved in the planning—providing you with ideas and information about:

What is being done.

What can be done.

What should be done.

What might be done.

Milestone charts and communication plans benefit from the ideas of your subordinates. By enlisting others in these projects, you can encourage them to shoulder the burden and contribute ideas such as:

Finding ways to save time and money.

Detecting potential problems and opportunity.

Identifying areas to improve communication.

Making optional plans.

Developing effective strategies.

Practicing new skills.

When resources are in short supply, as they are today, survival depends on your ability to find skills in everyone. Simple visualizations, pictures, and charts are useful particularly when they help you to measure critical elements. A milestone chart on the wall can enable all employees to stay in touch with progress.

A reporting system enables you to watch out for trouble, frees you to pick up and act on the complex cues in your work environment, and to prepare for your high priority, high-tension moments. It is important to simplify what you can, because the ambiguity at work makes the job complicated. Important problems do not yield to simple solutions. Despite techniques such as Bayesian and investment analysis, queuing theory, linear programming, and PERT, there are no adequate creative problem-solving tools for today's manager. Most of us are more skilled in analytic and judgmental problem solving. Our real decisions are, however, not routine; the information is unstructured. There is no simple formula for diagnosing an unstructured problem. The ever increasing complexity is, at times, bewildering and bothersome. There is no time to think about it all.

It is impossible to find enough uninterrupted time to devote to the major projects. Our moments are separated, disjointed, cut, and uneven. If you let them, your ideas can be chopped to pieces and your sentences separated from each other. You pick up a project at midpoint, advance it slightly and then go to a meeting where you defend what you worked on yesterday. Next you go on to work on another part of the first project. What you should do in an hour is accomplished in ten bits of ten minutes each.

In the early days of filmmaking, many actors found it difficult to switch from the continuous action of the stage to the chopping and piecing of the film. The director might do a two-and-a-half-minute scene in thirteen camera takes spread out over a whole day. This required actors to develop new techniques. They had to keep the structure of the action in mind despite the distractions, the fear of the mechanical contraptions surrounding them, and the pauses for lunch, to move the lights, or to wipe the brow. They had to know the action of the script by heart. Through concentration and observation they learned how to interrupt themselves without losing sight of the main event. Actors define the whole action within themselves. A mere hint and their technique allows them to do whatever is necessary. They move comfortably from role to role. They have collected many memories of what they do and of what others do. This collection provides experience, precision, economy, and enables them to achieve what they want. The director expects them to learn quickly and to remember.

Similarly, you need to know your action by heart. With a picture of the ideal structure, the main events, the tree with its straight proportioned trunk, you have a start. You can combine the secondary actions, interpret your vision to others, put your ideas and action together to achieve your goal.

With that plan—the action—clear in your mind, you can find ways to make it easier to move forward:

Plan small steps.
Practice.
Reinforce progress.

Delegate.

Reward achievement.

Find ways to use technology effectively, to advance activities, and to enhance capabilities and skills.

Your efforts in observation and concentration enable you to experience self-control as you keep your eye on the main events, do what has to be done, and limit yourself or take on new goals as appropriate. This will show itself in better management of the particles, the small bits of time. You will be able to identify and have time to fight the real fires and to prevent fires. Four questions can get you to the heart of the matter:

What exists?

What should exist?

Is the difference between the two important?

How do I know?

As a manager, you are essentially a pattern-making machine. Instead of needing fewer fragments and simpler pieces I find that I need more fragments, more complexity, and better questions. To deal with constant change, you need new bits of information, more ideas, and new approaches to your problems. Innovation is the result of new combinations of old fragments, shards, and bits of information. This requires an ever larger stock of fragments and the capacity to form new combinations and relationships.

Many managers attribute their success to systematic information gathering. You need to know everything that you can about your tasks, your customers, and your product. This includes specifications of products, rules—the routine and necessary parts of the job. Bernice Fitzgibbon of advertising fame ("Nobody but nobody undersells Macy's") admonished her copy writers: "Never write what you ain't saw." She insisted on seeing the curtains, plumping the pillows, tasting the tarts. Her advice extends to businesses beyond advertising. None of us knows enough. We need intimate knowledge of our businesses—brush-up courses on finance, programs on word processing equipment for executives, information on new products. Today many employees and managers work in offices remote from the end product. They lose touch with the big picture, with what the organization makes, with whom they serve. People at corporate headquarters may never see the toasters, shampoo, or tractors made by their companies. Government executives may get lost in policy development and congressional inquiries and forget that launching the payload in space is their objective. Thousands of university employees never know any students. The hospital's labor relations director may never see a patient.

You need to get out and gather information. Meet those in other areas of the work. Seek out books and journals of your industry. There are trade magazines in every field from shoe repair to astrophysics. It is easier to feel that you are part of the Space Shuttle after you have held one of the insulating tiles in your hand. "Show and tell" does help. An administrator assigned as director of operations at a small plant far from headquarters discovered that no one knew what was made in the other divisions. Her plant was scheduled to test a new product made by the major unit. She was concerned that the tests would be inadequately supported by her management and colleagues. Only she, fresh from headquarters, seemed to be aware that the testing was a high priority of top management. Her successful campaign to enlist support began with pictures of products from the other divisions, models of the product that would be tested, and films from all over the organization. She arranged for videotapes of the product to be shown on a local television evening news program.

You can never assume that people know enough, or that you know enough. You could make a point of recording your small bits of data on file cards. Indexing and cross-indexing your information helps you keep track of what you know, enables you to find gaps in your knowledge, and forces you to put your ideas in order (see Figure 10).

In gathering more fragments, you want to use and develop the skill of browsing. Many managers cite the value of reading widely outside the field. An important attribute of Conan Doyle's character Sherlock Holmes was his collection of scrapbooks in which

What do I need to know more about?

What do I want to know more about?

Sources of information:

Who:

What:

Where:

When:

How:

Figure 10. Gathering information.

he kept odd bits and pieces of information. Many mysteries were solved and many new ideas were generated when he studied, worked over, and browsed through this storehouse. Many managers and writers keep journals. The observations in Emerson's journal about watching someone peel potatoes turned up years later in a philosophical essay. A phrase that pleases you may provide a memorable title or an idea for a report—if you remember. This is more likely to happen if you write it down. Schedule at least an hour or two each month for the library to mine, almost at random, for gold. You want to look for new ideas. You need to take new looks at old ideas and at both new and old opinions in order to stretch your mind. Browsing through a library or bookstore can enhance the process.

Building information sources seems difficult in times of advocacy journalism when it is hard to believe what you read. Reading a variety of journals and papers can widen your world and provide balance. Many managers find that the *Wall Street Journal* provides a fast overview, well written editorials, and insightful articles on people at work. The *New York Times* news, editorial, and Op Ed pages provide a guide to the liberal establishment. The *National Review* and the *New Republic* further diversify that view. Alternate among the weekly news magazines: *Time, Newsweek,* and *US News and World Report.* You can get other viewpoints and approaches from the "MacNeil-Lehrer Report" and Charles

Kuralt's "Sunday Morning," from the *Harvard Business Review*, and dozens of other journals and newsletters. The trick is to avoid addiction to any single source of information.

You may want to keep your fragments and clippings in files, in a source book of ideas, or in scrapbooks à la Sherlock Holmes. You will have to work out your own way to organize the fragments. Some material is immediately useful. An economist interviewed on television may be the very person who could advise you and your financial planners. You may want to call him within the week. Other ideas can go into storage for a future improvement project. Some managers carry a notebook every day in which they record pertinent ideas and data, including phrases from their reading and quotations from meetings. One management trainer has collected pithy and wise phrases for years. Written boldly on newsprint, his "grafitti" paper the walls at his training sessions and provide a variety of ideas for the managers to think about.

Idea production is difficult to understand. The goal is to reconstruct some part of the world. It begins with your preoccupation with possibilities. "I dream of things that never were and say 'why not?'"

Effective management begins with the inability to leave well enough alone, with a preoccupation for betterment. This requires creating and controlling fragments. The principles and methods involved are simple, but learning them requires discipline and effort. "If you would lead, exert yourself" (Romans 16:4).

We recognize the difference between gathering ideas and transforming ideas into action. Discoveries about how the brain works by Nobel Prize winner Roger Sperry and his associates at the California Institute of Technology are beginning to illuminate that dual process. This group has, in a series of ingenious tests, revealed the separate functions of the two halves of the brain—the left and right hemispheres—and of the corpus collosum, the thick nerve cable that connects the two cerebral hemispheres. The verbal or left hemisphere appears dominant, but research indicates that the nonverbal side, the right half, merely processes information differently. Jerre Levy's studies showed that the right brain works in a visual, spatial, holistic manner. This processing is equal in complexity to the left brain's verbal and analytic mode. She found indications that the two modes interfere with one another or may work on several levels simultaneously. Investigation into the process of unstructured problem-solving suggests that at times we concentrate on left brain activity: linearity, time consciousness, and verbal logic; at other times we look at the total problem and are involved in right brain activity: synthesis, and intuitive, nonlogical processes. Although our education and culture often ignore right brain development, "scientific knowledge," as Robert Ornstein has pointed out, although "largely a linear and rational pursuit, also relies heavily on intuition for completeness."

The unstructured management situation is often characterized by fragmentation and fuzziness. We yearn in vain for a straight, logical answer. Our intuition of how we might solve the problem, the faint glimmerings of useful ideas, is our first step, what Jerome Bruner calls "the forging of metaphoric hunch into testable hypothesis." We then interpret and translate the results of our intuition, check its validity, and register it in a form that we can accept and that can be accepted by others.

The intuitive, relational thinking associated with the right brain has generally been ignored in our society. It appears to be increasingly essential that we learn to better use the right side of the brain for the ambiguous situations of our Future Shock world. The steps for unstructured problem-solving involve utilization of both the left and right brain—the two modes of conscious thought. We seem to alternate between the two modes. At our best, we select the appropriate one and inhibit the other.

The process begins with your organizing fragments into some sort of amorphous shape (see Figure 11). To turn this into useful ideas and actions, you gather and analyze your information. You might be trying to sell an idea or a new product, find a technological answer, design a system, write a policy, or explain a concert.

When routine responses do not work, you need to review and analyze your specific information to be certain that you have all the data that you need—check against Rudyard Kipling's famous serving men: why, what, who, when, where, how.

Synthesis of your odd bits of knowledge can enable you, in time, to find new solutions. Partial ideas and phrases that flit through your mind may be clues. Writing them down helps you to be more precise. This, of course, creates more fragments. Try to put ideas into new combinations. You could make a "bubble

LEFT BRAIN	RIGHT BRAIN
1. Assess overall situation.	
	2. Form vague picture.
3. Gather data, sequence, analyze information, organize ideas.	
	4. Form fragments into new patterns, synthesize data.
5. Review information and outline options.	
	6. Incubate, Eureka, Solution.
7. Clarify plan, figure costs, write out steps.	
	8. Present plan.

Figure 11. Working out solutions.

diagram" on a large piece of paper, perhaps using a flip chart and newsprint, putting your main event in the center and drawing a bubble around it. You add other thoughts as they rush through your mind, and capture them in your own shorthand phrases (see Figure 12).

Some managers work with different colors of felt pens or crayons at this stage of the process. This helps them to see the total situation and often provides insights into a need for more information or indicates new relationships.

Your diagram can often be quickly organized into an outline (see Figure 13). You will probably have new information bits as well. You can put them on cards, in file folders, or in a notebook. When you think that you have run out of ideas, look over everything again. Push yourself to create more fragments. Your objective at this point is not to solve the problem but to be certain that you have the best raw material on which to make decisions and to take action.

When you are designing a plan or working on a solution, there is a point when you need to let the ideas incubate. It is impossible to say how much preparation is necessary before incubation. One manager struggling to design a new program believed that he had considered every angle, read everything pertaining to his program, and addressed all the principles. A colleague's chance remark caused him to realize that he had overlooked another department's covetous interest in his work. Without their cooperation his effort could be stopped. If he had persisted in finding an answer without that information, he would have solved the wrong problem.

The paradox, of course, is that you can never have enough information, but you cannot gather information forever. At some point, you must move to incubation. You have to set aside the project and do something else. Go to a movie, watch television, read about an unrelated subject, take a walk, sleep, listen to music. Reading often gives me new insights. Some managers find that reading mysteries is helpful. The detective's elegant solution of a sticky situation absorbs them and gives them the confidence that they, too, will make order out of their bit of chaos. For a long time, we have known that passing time plays a role.

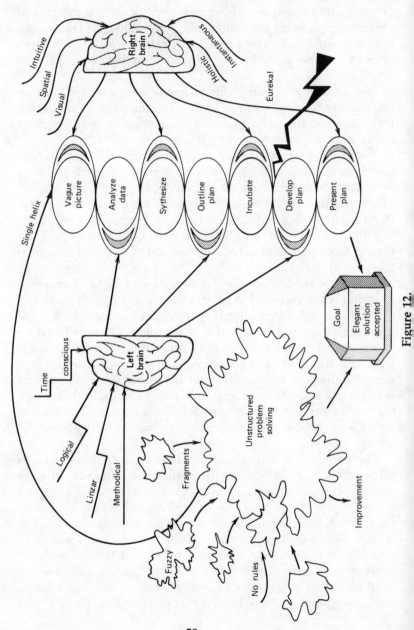

Figure 12.

You may have experienced the old adage of learning to swim in winter and skate in summer. At some points most of us have said, "Let me sleep on it." Our brains and body need time to assimilate theory and practice and to turn faltering steps into skills.

After rest and relaxation, and we return to our task, we find that the ideas, the old fragments, can be shaped into a new order.

Objective
    Betterment and innovation

Characteristics
    Complexity, no rules
    Vague, fragments, fuzzy.

Research on Left and Right Brain Provides Clues
    Left brain
        Logic, analysis, linear, verbal, methodical,
        in time
    Right brain
        spatial, visual, intuitive, holistic, synthesis,
        instantaneous.
    Need to integrate both modes.

Process
    "See" problem/Right brain
    Analyze data/Left brain
    Synthesize patterns/Right brain
    Outline ideas/Left brain
    Incubate ideas/Right brain

                    EUREKA

    Develop plan/Left brain
    Make presentation/Right brain

Figure 13. Working outline derived from bubble chart (Figure 12): Unstructured problem solving.

This is the basic method of innovation. This next step requires us to work the issues and make the ideas, the pieces, fit the exigencies of our world. At times, the best solution is not the one that we can implement. It may be too costly in money, time, or energy. People's pride may be adversely affected. Patience and practicality have their parts to play.

The last step requires you to share your ideas with others and obtain their reactions. If it is a good idea, it will grow. Others will be stimulated and will add to it from their ideas, from the fragments of their worlds. Rehearse it with those you respect. They will help you prevent surprises. Their additions can stimulate further ideas and shape your plan or idea to a state of practical usefulness. Their ideas can help you plan strategies for your main event, consider options, and ascertain costs. They can aid you in rehearsing your presentation.

We invariably tend to contrast the alienated or disengaged late—twentieth-century person with the whole person of some earlier paradise. The sense of fragmentation that our technology is supposed to have, and may have created, may be less of a problem than we suppose. A person today can realize his or her identity according to many functions, many roles, can create a fuller destiny than could people in those supposedly simpler times. This may be hard to bear. There are so many opportunities, so many choices, and so much going on that it is not surprising when people tend to forget the targets. The busyness can distract us from the elusive work of shaping the main event.

When we think seriously about it, there is no basic incompatiability between our sense of self and the many roles that we play. In fact, the capacity to gather new information, learn new skills, move from the role of disturbance handler to spokesperson to decision maker may be a desirable and enjoyable talent. Managers often report that they are intrigued and absorbed by the present times and their possibilities. Our industrial and electronic technologies bring more possibilities for maturity and freedom. Technology is our frontier. Our capacity for adaptation is the key to our turning fragments and fragmentation into possibilities.

Four

Some Days
the Dragon Wins

COPING WITH UNCERTAINTY

Fortune favors the man who keeps his nerve.
BEOWULF

Life has a way of not coming out even.
MIRIAM GROSOF

Your aim may be a harmonious pattern of parts working in sequence, but it is unlikely that you will achieve such stability. Unplanned and unwanted events can stop progress. A few unexpected events are providential and make us happy, but often, we encounter obstacles that make us miserable. On some days sheer survival is success enough. Jimmy the Greek says that life is eight to five against. In many periods of our life, it seems much worse. We take three steps back for each step forward.

Sometimes there is little we can do. Few of us are free to do whatever we want. Heads of organizations are accountable to shareholders, trustees, the electorate. In its own way red tape is real. In 1970, Marvin Weisbord posed the question in *Think* magazine, "What in your organization prevents you from doing as good a job as you know how to do?" If you ask that question, the answers may overwhelm you. There are many obstacles: limited influence, crisis managers, regulations, reduction in staff and budget, responsibility without authority, unreasonable demands. You could ask that question of those who work for you. I have been asking for more than ten years, and the answers always give me new dragons to fight.

Some work places are stressful and make people want to leave. To someone who experiences the work place as a prison, it does little good to say that stress is external. Maybe stress is what we make of it, but that can be difficult to understand or to live with. His Eskimo friend chided Edmund Carpenter, the anthropologist, "The wind is not cold, you are cold." That sounds fine and philosophical. Maybe the wind is not cold, but when the north wind is blowing, it is hard for the shorn lambs to be warm. If you are in a place that is stressful, you are affected, and you affect that place. Often people distort themselves to remain in a place or system or to keep it together. If your work place is chaotic, you may have to leave or simply resign yourself to feeling bad. Sometimes you can make no sense out of a system because it is organized to be crazy. This is never fun. It is unpleasant when someone else places painful pressures on you. You may feel that there is little you can do.

If you are waiting for a fairy godmother to fix it, you are waiting in vain. You are sitting in a well. You can either decorate the walls and tell people droll stories of how you happen to be living in a well or you can start to climb out.

When you are having a really bad time of it, listen to your stomach. Concentrate on how you feel. Sometimes a review of your situation, from boat payments to the orthodontist's bill, indicates that what is important is to have a regular paycheck. If you feel that you must stay where you are, figure out what you could learn or accomplish in a specific period of time. Work hard. Be as first-rate as possible. Perhaps you can make small changes that make your present position possible.

You could clarify how the situation affects you. Conflict can lead to new ideas. If someone opposes you, that person gives you an opening. It is worse and more common to meet silent opposition. No one tells you that anything is wrong. They may deny that anything is wrong even when you ask them. They may even say "yes" to your ideas but do nothing. This leaves you nowhere. If they oppose your ideas, you are, at least, involved in an active consideration of your position. You could make clear to them what changes must take place if you are to remain on the job. This entails risk, for you must be prepared to leave. The alternative is that you may have to go on hoping for something that may never happen. You may have to accept that fact there is no hope for change.

Blaming others promotes passivity and is a way back to the well. Regardless of who is at fault, it is up to you to take it from here. In a passive-conflict situation, productivity declines. Since you are responsible for your own actions, recognize your own role in less-than-perfect situations. This is when things can start to get better.

Do what you can. Examine what you are doing. Make things easy on yourself. Life is hard, and some days seem to be endless doldrums. They pass. When you feel trapped and can see nothing in any direction, try to see why you feel that way. No one goes through the employment process unscathed, but be wary of complaining without taking action. It is not necessary to like everything about a place or a job. We all do many things that we would prefer not to do. Think how much time you spend doing things not of your choice. What changes are in your power?

The more you act in your own behalf, the better you will feel.

In adverse situations, it is important to keep the main event in mind. Watch your own actions with as much objectivity as you can. Be especially careful to set yourself goals for development and understanding, and set aside time each day to work toward their achievement. If you can, ascertain how the objectives of your supervisor can fit into your evolving career plan.

It is especially hard to deal with change when it is for the worse. The literature tends to assume that change is progress or that new situations will be better. This view further assumes that subordinates need to be "sold" because they are lazy and prefer the comfortable old ways. The implication behind this assumption is that supervisors know better than their employees. If you are a manager instituting change that others may or may not welcome, recognize that you may not know best. Your employees may be right. The change may be a rotten idea. You can figure that people will at least accept change when:

The purpose is clear.
Their interests are served.
Their work habits are respected.
Communication is good.
They are part of the planning.
Reward will be forthcoming, not punishment.
The present situation is inadequate.

People do not accept change when its purpose is unwise, against their self-interest, or punishing. As a manager, you may have to implement a reorganization whose purpose is unclear or which involves undesirable actions. You and your employees, working together, can mitigate some of the unpleasantness. Try to make the purpose clear and endeavor to alter anything that will make the working situation more pleasant. Accelerating societal change, today, often results in reorganization. This disturbs the status quo, threatens people's security, and upsets established procedures (see Figure 14).

Communicate the nature of the change:

People
Basis of decisions
Timing
Options
Ground rules
Unknowns

Demonstrate confidence.

Acknowledge potential anxiety.

Accept feelings of betrayal.

Involve everyone in planning.

Think about changes and related activities daily.

Review plans and information regularly.

Move quickly.

Reinforce progress.

Figure 14. Preparing employees for unwanted change.

A bookstore manager, told to cut his budget by 20%, obtained agreements from some employees to work part-time, help him work out new cut-rate sources, and eliminate various supplies. They cut the budget by 22% and expected further saving due to attrition at summer's end when some employees would return to school. He was shocked to be told that his budget cutting was inadequate because no one was fired. He diverted attention and stalled for two months. A few employees left. His only problem then was that he lacked people to cover the peak fall period. Even with overtime, he managed to stay within his budget by attending daily to sales and expenses. Despite enormous stress, he, his operation, and employees survived.

Work is what we make it. If it is based on fear, if it induces alienation, if it punishes creativity, it is not doing what it should. The activities of work can be changed. It is easier to change work than to change people.

Whereas reorganizations are seldom failures, few are truly successful. Companies report that moderate reorganization is a yearly occurrence. This is expensive in time and energy. Managers initiating change recognize but fail to assess the resistance that employees can offer. There will be some who see personal advantage in a reorganization. Others, easily bored, will enjoy the novelty. A few may work aggressively to undermine the reorganization, but more will resist passively. Employees with a low tolerance for change may fear that they are losing something of value. You can ease the situation by reassuring and encouraging such employees during difficult changes. You could look for things that different employees do well. Your recognition of small successes will encourage development and tolerance of change.

In a reorganization, managers face a negotiating period. What is happening is that the psychological contract has been changed. You need a new one. All too often, instead of negotiating, managers choose to exhort or educate. This misses the mark. These are usually the answers to a different question. It is better to determine a new contract.

There is no way for you to obtain enough information to make an adequate analysis of the situation. To deal with those who resist the reorganization, you will have to live with ambiguity and inaccuracy. If you do not work from where they are, real improvement may be held up and new programs put off.

Some managers, facing resistance, push ahead, fire people, and institute their plans anyway. The jungle fighter who behaves this way is an endangered species whom no one will miss. Such people breed hostility, turning indifferent colleagues and subordinates into pained adversaries and, even enemies. Making enemies is a poor idea. One never knows where someone will turn up again or in what position. Some people will not like you no matter what you do. You can prevent those who are neutral from joining your enemies. No one needs a surplus of enemies. They make life difficult. If you have to spend your time protecting yourself, this could prevent you from doing the job that will win you an "Emmy" or an outstanding leadership award. Enemies only clutter your life and clutter kills.

Sometimes you may be on the other side of a reorganization, being reorganized rather than reorganizing. The prospect may be disquieting. Your scope limited, you acquire a boss whom you would not choose, you have new and less desirable assignments. You may be moved to an inconvenient office with limited access to information, a smaller staff, and less money. At the very least, reorganization can affect your productivity. It slows people down. Knowing that you are not alone will not make this better, but even in an unpleasant situation you can find positives and pleasures that help you to regain control over your work environment.

In a merger of any kind, there will be uneasiness on all sides. If you are the weakest player in the merger, the more powerful side will be worried about your reaction. Following Philip Crosby's advice: Make a point to smile and listen quietly while you gather ideas and information. You should answer questions truthfully, avoid all negative comments, and refrain from volunteering information. You can busy yourself taking thoughtful notes. It is important that you think in terms of *us* and *we*, not *us* and *them*.

By being friendly when hostility is expected, you can more easily get *them* to understand what you are about. You need to communicate what is important. If you can show a new supervisor that you will make him or her look good, you can get back to tackling your own key career objectives.

After a merger, the main event may be solidifying your position in line with your organization's goals and objectives. This may seem difficult if promotion opportunities are cut off or if you are in danger of losing your job. Yet in this negative situation, you can find an unparalleled opportunity to set the stage so that your performance is perceived as you want it to be perceived. You are subject to negative evaluation, especially if your organization knows little about your work. Never assume that they know what you do. They probably have very little idea of what you do. This can lead them to think that you don't do much. Your aim is to have them see you as a valuable person who can contribute to the organization. It is important that you be perceived as a positive force.

If you are downgraded because your skills are no longer valuable to the organization, consider getting into a new field. Invest in learning new skills. Maybe the organization will train you. You could begin to add onto your duties as people retire or change jobs. I have seen managers regain their former glory this way. Should your duties and staff be reduced, this could give you the time to consider new goals or acquire new knowledge. A demotion may, however, be a strong warning; ignoring it will not make it go away.

Reorganizations and mergers are never as well organized as we'd like. There are cracks for tasks to fall into, unmapped territories, new roles, and jobs to be created. By being alert to the opportunities while everyone else is moaning about problems, you may pick up ideas that will help you get on with some of your goals. You may be able to learn new skills or launch an important project.

Keep a file drawer or large notebook of untimely and rejected proposals. This repository of "Future Improvement Projects" can include newsclippings, fragments, and ideas that intrigue you. When you make a proposal that is rejected, save it. When you must kill off a pet project, save your notes. Its time may come. If you keep running through your stock, alert to the conditions, you may find that a merger is the perfect time to dust off a budget system for which your previous management had no time. This could be the moment to propose a new product, a research project, or a sales campaign.

If it is ten o'clock in the morning and you are ready for lunch, your first thought may be to redo your resumé and check the classified section of the newspaper. This may be appropriate, but it could be easier and more effective to go through your store of Future Improvement Projects for ideas and suggestions.

One way to determine what may be possible is to initiate a discussion with your supervisor to discuss his or her vision and goals for the organization. Try to learn what specific projects or products will be initiated or maintained. Your task is to "seek to understand your manager's alignment" as Culbert and McDonough say. Your aim is to make it clear that you understand what he or she is trying to accomplish. Ask questions carefully so that you develop a highly detailed picture. Look for values, themes, and projects that will carry out the management's theme. Find out what territories are open. Express your interests in terms of excellence of project, previous achievements, and related experience. You can talk about your skills and interest as they relate to the organization's mission. You can let your supervisor know what you want to accomplish, but it is often unwise to be too specific in terms of a job. What is best for you may not be best for them. If you back your supervisor into a corner, you will be resented. Decisions will be made on the basis of their values and interests. You need to be seen as *one of us* not *one of them*. That will not happen overnight. You may lose the initial battle but try to include your new supervisor as an ally in your life. As does Charlie Brown, we "need all the friends we can get."

Your good ideas may have to be returned again and again to your Future Improvement Projects file. You may be better off if you don't win too easily or too early. On the other hand, you need some success if you are to maintain the momentum that will enable you to conceive and carry out the plans for Camelot.

If you are careful, you may be lucky. One manager threatened with dismissal in a large organizational merger suggested a personnel representative plan to the new vice-president for human resources. The plan had been developed a year earlier but the timing had been wrong. Suddenly the threat of a union drive provided the impetus for installing the system. It proved to be a success. Managers from sixty major units met monthly, learned about their personnel responsibility, and took an active role in developing policies to prevent labor problems. Their questions and concerns caused the manager to reach into her Future Improvement Projects stock for an orientation program for supervisors and new employees. Both of these projects enhanced her new vice-president's position. Instead of being fired, the manager was promoted.

Things do not always work out so well. There are no easy answers when an important piece of your job is given to someone else to bolster his or her position description, when someone else gets credit for work that you do, or you get turned down over and over on projects that are important to you. One manager told me of a successful art program that he had developed and produced for several years for his company. The profit was respectable. School principals and students alike praised his work. While he was working on the fourth edition, another office suddenly claimed that the project required their approval. He had to submit the text to them and spend his time explaining his pedagogy and punctuation. Discouraged, he dropped the whole idea. Everyone knows someone with a story like that.

The paradox is that, as R. G. H. Sui states, you must expect "foul play" and believe at the same time in the words of Carl Rogers: "The facts are friendly." Should you see someone kick the cat—thinking that no one is looking—watch out. No one should willingly work for someone who is mean. Do not stay to be kicked yourself.

You may miss the warnings and be surprised by an unexpected attack. Someone in a meeting or conference might launch an unreasonable tirade or react to you with outrageous and inappropriate anger. You may get the bad news that your job is being changed or eliminated. You may be publicly embarrassed, blamed for something that you did or did not do. Someone may rip you, your work, or your reputation to shreds. You may be threatened with some adverse job action. You may be told that you are getting a new boss with a reputation for violent and sadistic behavior. Your reaction will vary according to the situation, your experience, the environment. If you stop and check your feelings, you may find that you are afraid. Fear usually shows. That's all right. Several elements are involved: you, the person who is attacking you, and the environment. Start by focusing on what you want and how you want to behave. You are responsible for your actions. If you lose your composure, you are not going to be able to control your reaction. The task is to stay in touch with your feelings but act in your self-interest. Otherwise, as George Peabody states, you will react out of your feelings.

If the attack is a real shock and you feel dazed, continue to look that way for a moment. Try to keep your mouth closed. Think. When you are attacked, your most important action can be to stand still. It is best to do nothing but think. What can you get out of this situation? It may be that you have some options: asking for a review, calling in old debts, filing a grievance, requesting a transfer, asking for help, rallying support, filing a suit. Try to see the person who attacked you as a human being. That may be very difficult. Look for something good: appearance, strength, clothing, voice, intelligence—anything. Try to gain confidence. The real action in an attack will be your reaction. If someone is telling you bad news, he or she is probably nervous about how you will act. Stall until you can gain control. Use your imagination and judgment. There is no standard technique or answer.

In a bad situation, stop and ask yourself, "What do I need to do in order to behave in the manner that I prefer?" This could mean that you need to get away. The world will not end if you stand and say "Excuse me. I'll be back shortly." You must move quickly out the door and leave it open behind you. You must be calm. Decisiveness is the key. If you ask for permission with words, gesture, or tone of voice, you've lost. They may wonder what you are up to but that is their problem. You do not have to take punishment. If you go for a walk, punch a pillow, yell, call your lawyer, your therapist, or a supportive friend, that could help. In a bad situation, it matters that you stay in control, remain aware of what is happening and avoid self-destructive behavior. I have seen people who have lost control burst blood vessels and worse. This is no time to get drunk, to take pills, to punch someone, or break the furniture. Your main events remain your own personal plans, your self-interest, accomplishing your goals. Recognize in an unpleasant situation that you are in pain. Keep before you a clear picture of your self-interest. Act on that interest and not on your understandable desire to get even. Remember the Spanish adage: Living well is the best revenge.

When sheer survival is success, recognize that you are in a stressful situation. Take care of yourself, enjoy physical exercise and other pleasures, and expand your knowledge and skills in listening, assertiveness, and conflict techniques.

Tension is inherent in the ways you perceive and deal with these events. You may be able to improve your situation merely by recognizing the sources of petty irritations and by working out new ways to deal with them. If you usually react angrily when your boss overreacts to a situation, you could try a new approach.

Whereas expressing anger is important, it is inappropriate to fight over everything.

When you feel yourself becoming anxious you could say "No," sit quietly, take a minute to enjoy the world. You need to test and know the conditions under which you perform well. Some people work best under pressure of deadlines; others freeze. If you know what feels good to you and how those feelings correlate with performance, you can pace yourself effectively. As you balance performance with satisfaction, you can improve your own luck.

You can learn from actors to block out insecurity, especially in high tension moments when you, too, are on stage. Like Jiminy Cricket, you may find a happy tune that brings your spirits up. A world-famous film actress, terrified of public appearances, put herself in the role of her acting group's operations manager. The woman had to rise to her feet every day and admonish a roomful of actors for their poor housekeeping, cajole them to wash coffee cups, and discard sandwich wrappings in the trash bin. Recognizing that this was a necessary but unpleasant task, the actress noted how the other woman used humor and accurate observation to deal with each day differently. Later, when reporters trapped the actress, picturing that scene enabled her to respond to the same old questions with humor, accurate observation, and freshness. Although her fear remained, she told the manager that she felt more confident and sometimes, even, courageous.

Some crises cannot be avoided and in fact, can provide exhilaration because of your increased importance. You have to react very quickly to trouble. This can even happen to very good managers because none of us can anticipate all of the consequences of everyone's actions every single day. As in *Macbeth*, troubles seem to come "not single spies but in battalions." It could be that you were wrong. If so, like Bobby Fisher, regard defeat as a fluke. Admit your error and see what you can do to make sure it never happens again. You can expect problems at certain times: when you start a new program, modify a production model, change suppliers, renovate the building, find yourself in the middle of a flu epidemic, or the holiday period. You can alleviate some pain through planning and scheduling. You can't make the products, the project or the people perfect.

When disaster strikes, you will just have to stop and develop short-term solutions. Sometimes there is nothing you can do, for example, a person in another department can stop your subordinate from getting a cash award that you recommended, by suggesting that it is undeserved. You may not know about the conversation until it is too late. Your proposal can be stymied in committee by someone with no knowledge of your work. Sometimes the person who messes up another person's project does so because he or she is bitter and has lost interest in the organization.

A little perspective helps. A manager who received a threatening telephone call from a former employee feared that the threat was real. He happened to be in the office alone and called the security office. The officer told him to leave the office and visit a friend while he did some investigating. Later the manager realized that he thought his job was to stay and face the situation. *High Noon* was a movie. It was crazy to sit there in the empty office startled by every sound. "Other duties as assigned" does not include dealing with threats of violence. If it's part of your job description, it will be spelled out. In films of terror, victims tend to sit in their homes frightened by weird phone calls, bizarre notes, and other hoodlum activity. Such films may even promote passivity and inaction.

If the resistances at work are strong and numerous it is difficult to see how you can accomplish your goals. You know that almost anything is possible. "How" is the trick. The problem is time. It can take so much effort to go through or under or around that you become worn out. You may have to ask yourself if the situation is worth the effort. This is one reason that I keep saying: "Keep your eye on the main event."

Few of us have a wide repertoire of conflict skills. Almost everyone knows about "fight" and "withdrawal." We can argue, yell, and pound the table. We can decide not to do anything. Either can, in its own way, be dangerous and lead to win–lose situations in which the odds are tipped heavily against you. Your goal is a win–win situation. This calls for skill. You can try to compromise, accommodate, or collaborate on a solution. If it's really a painful situation, you probably feel that you have accommodated long enough. Collaboration is the quality solution; however, it takes time and requires the cooperation and willingness of others. This may be impossible. Compromise can be less than you deserve but the best that you can do under the circumstances.

An overburdened manager was pressed to take on new and risky assignments. He was unsure of his vice-president's motives. Remembering the claim of Delmore Schwartz, that paranoiacs have enemies too, he elected to act as if his management wanted him to win. He looked around the organization and found a bright, underemployed secretary. He asked to have her assigned parttime to his projects so that he could concentrate on what he was hired to do and could get fired for. He made a good case for increased productivity. Because this compromise solution was not costly, it was accepted. His problems were not solved but he gained time for planning, and enlisted the secretary as an ally. She suggested ways to complete some of the tedious tasks and managed to find another secretary to help them in a crunch. They solved several troublesome problems and made significant progress on others. Their productivity was high. He, at least, saved his sanity, achieved goals that mattered to the organization, and improved his negotiating position.

Too often, a manager succeeds in making an employee look bad. A newly appointed vice-president, an old jungle fighter, made no secret of his plans to destroy three of his directors. One, a food director, had recently opened, to high praise, a beautiful rooftop restaurant. He was rebuilding two kitchens and overseeing ten successful establishments. The vice-president harassed him with unreasonable demands. The director became defensive and hostile when questioned about turnover, menus, and safety. He began to incur cost overruns on his remodeling projects. In six months he had an ulcer and found his world so muddled that he took the blame when a bitter trucker's strike hobbled his projects. In an angry confrontation one afternoon, he resigned and no one ever heard from him again.

The company's labor relations director was an obvious target for barbs about his inefficiency as a manager. He was a brilliant negotiator but his real value to the corporation was the effectiveness with which he administered the contract. He recognized that he would be better off in a smaller organization where he could deal directly with negotiation and contract implementation. He did not enjoy delegation or managing a staff. Eight years later he is happy in a small company where his staff consists of one secretary. He now enjoys his relations with the company president, the union, and the workers. He has time to write several articles a year on labor relations for law journals and to teach arbitration and mediation in a local law school. His focus saved his health and his happiness.

The third director had several projects that he wanted to complete. Because of prior successful work for the president and several other vice-presidents, he had the strongest base of the three directors. His programs in real estate and construction were tied closely to the organization's pressing and visible problems. He was seen as someone whose work straddled boundaries between the organization's units and the outside world. He kept his contacts with people in key positions who respected him as a skillful manager of risky areas. He carefully killed off projects that did not serve his purposes and took on nothing new. Taking his time, he achieved the results that he wanted and used that success to get a new and better job.

In most organizations, the food director's story is the most familiar. It need not be. Be wary of defensiveness when you sense criticism. If your supervisor has an idea to improve your division—which does not necessarily mean that you are doing something wrong—don't defend yourself. As my grandmother always said, "Never explain, your friends do not need it and your enemies will not believe you anyway." You can use a technique of assertiveness training called "fogging," which can be useful with people who attack unfairly or offer gratuitous criticism. To unkind remarks and attacks you simply say, "Some people might say that," "Thank you for your comment," or "I appreciate your concern." Such responses can be useful additions to your management skills. They enable you to keep your eye on the main event. "Fogging" prevents escalation of unpleasant emotions and enables you to retain control in order to continue your work.

Eli Djeddah suggests that on arriving home we should immediately describe the two most wonderful things that happened, such as "I had a great day, no one hit me." The practice of finding positives in negative situations is strengthening. Despair is human but your best interest is served if you show—even unfelt—confidence and courage.

If your supervisor's world view is at odds with your own, you need to determine how much this will affect your relationship. If your values are challenged, keep in touch with your personal themes. If morality is the issue, you might find a way to do some extra work. For example, if your supervisor makes racist and sexist remarks and you are a working minority woman or simply have strong feelings on this subject, you might offer to take responsibility for equal opportunity in the office, or to monitor contractor compliance. This serves many purposes: It adds legally and socially mandated responsibilities, introduces you to new people and experiences, and allows you to remain true to personal beliefs. You will develop expertise in another field, relieve your boss of unfavored work, and improve your organizational posture.

One executive advises that you never think about any difficulty after 10 p.m. She says that if you must, do no more than make a list of nine possible solutions. Often what seems to be the least useful suggestion turns out, in the comfort of daylight, to be your best solution. The important thing is that you form the habit of orderly thinking.

Another executive told me that when a problem leads to insomnia, he turns on the light and writes down the facts as he knows them. Then he numbers them in importance. Finally he imagines how other people might see the situation. In particular, he tries to project how someone he doesn't like or who doesn't approve of him would describe what is happening.

What usually emerges is that he doesn't know the facts well enough to proceed. If he feels that he needs important information, his goal for the next day is clear. He writes down what he must do.

Some conflicts are common and painful. If a co-worker steals your idea, it can be difficult to know what to do. This is where confrontation and active problem-solving can be appropriate. If you go to that person and say: "We both know that x was my idea. If we are going to work together, we had better figure out what we are going to do from now on." This is a difficult request for someone to ignore. Above all, do not panic. If you had a good idea once, it is likely that you will have one again.

As you expand your repertoire of techniques to handle conflicts, analyze your progress. Notice how much risk you are willing to take and how successful you are at keeping your options open. You can take control of the situation or wait for someone else to take control. In most situations, the person who stays in control will be the winner.

Sometimes the organization's very survival is at stake. If the competition is shooting you up or the city council is shooting you down, your big task is to reorder priorities. Saving money may move to the top of the list. This may be necessary, but if you have no other ideas, the organization will probably fail. Then the real question is, "Is the organization worth saving?" It may be that you are arranging deck chairs on the Titanic. If this is a temporary nadir, you want to identify the main events that can enable you to rise again. You need to take action to move forward, to make money, to gain support. You could, in the meantime, look for creative approaches to deploying your work force (see Figure 15). Such action needn't be limited to bad times.

If the staff must be cut, a placement program will not solve all of your problems, but it can help, as it enables employees to take better control of job hunting at a difficult time. This enables you to ease conflicts and counteract bitterness and poor morale in the organization.

It is no fun to fire people, but sometimes you must. Maybe you have to dismiss people because of sheer economics. Other times, you simply have problems with an employee.

Many managers have problem employees whose performance causes sleepless nights and daily pain. The situation worsens slowly and, in time, neither side will be blameless. Constructive discipline is a useful approach (see Figure 16).

The practice of constructive discipline first requires that you define the problem. You determine the discrepancy between the employee's performance and what is desired. If the discrepancy matters, you have the responsibility to let the employee know. You don't have to reproach the employee but you need to describe what the employee does and what you want. This information enables workers to measure and direct themselves. Most people, given information about their performance, will improve. This is particularly true if your feedback is timely, relevant, and an accurate description of your perception. If you intend this discussion to be a warning, present it as such, and

---

Train people for new skills.

Redesign jobs, shifting some tasks to other employees according to ability as attrition occurs.

Reduce work hours (with employee's cooperation).

Assign employees to reexamine all costs and expenditures.

Develop internal skill bank for special projects:
    New markets
    Service development
    Housekeeping.

Loan people to community projects, trade associations, government.

Cut back on perquisites but extend to more people those that are inexpensive.

Ask employees for suggestions on cutting waste and implement the best ones quickly.

Set goals for improvement and chart progress.

Figure 15.   Deployment of employees.

---

make it clear that you anticipate specific improved performance. For your own record, make notes of the conversation.

Sometimes you may have an employee who fails to respond to feedback. When appraisal fails, you have to warn the employee on his or her performance. This should be in writing, should refer to the previous discussion, detail your expectations, and warn that failure to improve could lead to further disciplinary action. Do not specify what action you will take. Leave yourself options.

All of us at various times can be depressed, defeated, indecisive, or confused. An employee who fails to respond at this point may be very troubled. This hurts our work and our relations with

---

Observe the employee at work.

Clarify the discrepancy between what
exists and what is desired.

Does it matter?

How do I know?

Could the person do better if
life depended on it?

Can the job be changed?

Talk with the employee and describe
both present behavior and changes desired.

In records, note date of conversation
with employee and expectations.

If no improvement, give the
employee a written warning:

Refer to previous meeting.

Describe expectations.

Describe what employee is doing.

Warn of further disciplinary action.

If no improvement, process
suspension with personnel office.

If no improvement, process discharge.

Figure 16. Constructive discipline.

others. To be effective with employees whose behavior troubles you, you have to feel very comfortable with yourself. You may then be able to help an employee solely because of your commitment and involvement. It may be enough if you can convey your interest in their concerns. With employees whose problems seem too difficult, professional help may be necessary. One occupational therapist suggests to managers that they recommend a physical checkup to a troubled employee because it will make him or her feel cared for. This could be therapeutic in itself. The employee might be able to accept a physician's recommendation for further therapy. Many managers find it easier to suggest a medical examination than to suggest psychological help. You could, of course, discuss the situation with a therapist yourself.

If, despite all this attention, there is no improvement, further discipline is necessary. Suspension is the next step. By this time, through feedback, and oral and written warning, you will have made it clear that there is a problem. Your organization may require that you consult with a personnel or labor relations officer before suspending or firing someone. It is a good idea.

Under a system of constructive discipline, you rarely have to fire anyone. Faced with the mismatch between their ability and the requirements of the job, most people realize that things are going badly and they resign. Despite provocation, it is unwise to fire anyone in anger. When employees who were arguing bitterly pulled knives on one another, their manager told the employees firmly that they were both suspended for three days and were to leave the premises immediately. To her relief, they left. If they had not, she could have called the security officials or the police. Fortunately, most managers have less exciting labor problems. Should you fire someone, avoid Friday afternoons. This gives people time to brood. Monday morning is not good but it is better. Prepare a written statement of the individual's rights, the financial settlement, information on insurance and other benefits, and what help you can give. People remember almost nothing mentioned in a termination interview. If you cannot, do not offer to write glowing references.

Analyze the case to see what you can do to be certain that the situation never repeats itself. When there is a weak link in your organization, that person or division will demand extraordinary attention and commitment of resources. The weakest subsystem will always dominate.

It may be that the weakest subsystem in your organization is your own supervisor. The situation may be impossible, the chemistry between you intolerable. One manager said that it took a double martini, two aspirins, and a hot bath each evening before her eyes uncrossed. This is trouble. Do not fool yourself that things will get better. The unemployment offices are filled with people who thought they would never lose their jobs.

If you are fired, that is a pretty terrible moment. Later you may decide that it was the best day of your life, but at that moment, it is terrible. You may have known it was coming. If not, you probably should have known. Often we delude ourselves and pretend that all is well. Many people miss obvious clues.

If you are fired, concentrate on getting as much help for the future as possible. Find out everything that you can about why you were fired and what signals you may have missed. They may be reluctant to tell you anything but ask gently and persistently. Let them know that you never want to make the same mistakes again. If they accuse you unjustly, refrain from creating an argument. You can say, "I do not see myself as you describe me." You need not accept their judgment. If they fail to follow proper procedures or if they behave in a manner that seems illegal or unethical, you can point out that you believe that their behavior is unfair—but save your arguments. Should pensions, stock options, or other financial settlements be at stake, don't sign any papers without checking with a lawyer. This sounds obvious but people often sign disadvantageous agreements in anger. Should you file a grievance, a complaint, or have further settlement discussions, you want to be sure that you have not jeopardized your position.

When you leave your termination interview and go back to your office—that is a tense moment. You face real work. There is no job so difficult as job hunting. If you have done it before, you know that it is. If this is a new experience, you will soon know. You need to make plans, to write and call people. You should have at your fingertips a good long list of people whom you have helped, who can now help you. You have new priorities. You must redefine your own main event, plan how to achieve your goals, and take action to see other people. Some can give you advice. Others will refer you to other people. There are those who can give you information about organizations. Some can recommend you for jobs, and somewhere there is a golden person who can hire you.

From her experience in the advertising business, where being fired is a common experience, Jane Trahey says that, should you be fired, there is little purpose in sitting in your office drowning in self-pity. She suggests that, instead, you go out for a haircut, buy, and wear back to the office an elegant new shirt or outfit. This enables you to avoid the gossip and questions and provides you with a constructive purpose. This is not frivolous. You need to look prosperous when you job hunt just as you must when asking for a bank loan. Then, looking wonderful, you can return, gather up your belongings and say goodbye—leaving them wondering why they are letting you go. That, as Hemingway said, is "grace under pressure."

You don't have to wait to be fired. There are lessons here for all of us. She also suggests that every so often you pretend that you have been fired. Every six months, you could rehearse what you would do. You try out different approaches, scripts, and speeches. Thinking through and practicing what you might do or say enables you to prepare yourself for life's surprises. It can be illuminating to discover what ideas that exercise releases (see Figure 17).

In our troubles, we can learn from Michael Chekov, a famous stage director, who said, "An actor should approach each part with a little contempt." This never means that the part is unimportant or that you can be careless or fail to make a total effort. Hard work and skill are important but what really matters is that the results are less important than your self-worth.

Should the dragon win, remember what Gertrude Stein said: "The way to resume is to resume."

What do I think my first actions would be?

Is that what I would want to do?

What could I do that would be more effective?

What are my assets and liabilities?

If I didn't have this job, what would I want to do?

If I know, why don't I do it?
What is stopping me?

If I don't know, what should I do to figure that out?

What would I do in the first week and month, if I were fired today?

What does this tell me that I might or should be doing now?

Figure 17.   What I would do if I were fired.

Five

A Tune Upon the Blue Guitar

EFFECTIVE COMMUNICATING AND LISTENING

Language is a map describing reality. It is not reality.
ALFRED KORZYBSKI

To feel as well as hear what someone says requires whole attention.
SYLVIA ASHTON-WARNER

I am the most spontaneous speaker in the world because every word, every retort has been carefully rehearsed.
GEORGE BERNARD SHAW

Communication—perception and presentation—is central to your ability to enlist others in your cause and advance the main event. This requires an understanding of communication as a bargaining process that takes place between:

What is reality and what you see as reality
Storyteller and listener
Idea and action

Oral communication is very complex and often obscures more than it reveals. Whatever is hidden is hidden from us when we try to present ideas as well as when we are trying to understand another person's ideas.

You have a lot to consider—a lot at stake. To turn your idea into action, you must tell someone about it. If you want to enlist others in your enterprise, you must ask for their help. When you are thwarted, you must muster allies and overcome opposition. To mobilize support and create unity of purpose, your task is to transfer information from your mind to another person's mind with a minimum of distortion.

Your presentation is, itself, a main event, a form of teaching. You must be an expert on your subject and, also, be very clear in your own mind about:

Your self-interest
The self-interest of your audience
What you want them to do when you are finished

If you say to someone, "I have an idea," watch his or her reaction very closely. Often the eyes will narrow slightly, the coloring change, and the breathing become shallow. These small signs of anxiety may be accompanied by the tapping of a pencil and, even, the question "What will it cost me?" When we have worked to develop an idea, or perhaps a good solution to a major problem, others will seldom accept it with the alacrity and enthusiasm we desire. Many managers find that their ideas are rejected without serious consideration. People often naively believe that all they have to do is lay out the facts and let the truth of their position carry the day. This does not happen.

Oral presentation is a test of leadership. It makes some people nervous. Only you can decide to what extent you are willing to dramatize your story. You have to determine what is appropriate with your audience, and if the ends justify the means. The line between persuasion and propaganda is invisible and, admittedly, thin.

As Wallace Stevens makes clear in the poem "A Tune Upon the Blue Guitar," to "tell of things exactly as they are" is no easy matter. The major pieces—what to say, how to say it, and to whom—fail to stay neatly in place. Marshall McLuhan's oversimplification, "the medium is the message," contains some truth. Slickness sells. Although what you say is more important than how you say it, style can matter more than substance. That's the paradox. Amateurism distracts, and hesitancy can shatter your efforts.

On most occasions, you can only tell part of the truth. The dangers in this are distortion, deletion of material, and self-delusion. Nothing must deflect you from trying to see the whole truth. You can seldom tell the truth, the whole truth, and nothing but the truth. We lack litmus tests on what truths are to be withheld. If you tell an incompetent employee the truth, he may be shattered. If you tell a client that her marketing practices are exploitive, you'll probably lose the account. You may be wrong. Timing is a factor. Telling everything that you know as soon as you know it can be a bad idea. Nonetheless, the issue is integrity. You will have to acquire the ability to accept the use of partial truths in relation to your main event. This is tricky, time-consuming, and risky. The effort that you must make to maintain vigil over the facts is a very good reason for you to delegate jobs to other people. They can draft your letters, sell the product, prevent problems. Keeping in touch with what should or shouldn't be disclosed is something that only you can do.

Manipulation is the worry. No one likes to be manipulated. Communication, with its hidden persuaders and the like, is dangerous. Ethics is the issue. We have seen the horrifying results of manipulative and exploitive communication. However, communication is not the villain. The culprits are villainous communicators.

Telling your story effectively can make a difference. Many executives, despite experience to the contrary, persist in believing that all they need to do is use sheer intellect, stating their ideas in a straightforward, logical fashion. They continue to be surprised when they fail. If they were testing a system that failed, they would review what they had done and what they should have done differently. When what you do fails to work, look for something else to do. Logic, intelligence, and analysis won't do the whole job.

Oral communication is a nonlogical process. It involves emotions, perceptions, and physical responses that we are only now beginning to understand. Our emotions are older than our intellects. The environment of a presentation is emotional, holistic, simultaneous, and intuitive. This is unsettling if you are trained and experienced in analytical, logical, sequential, and linear thought. Logic and analysis have roles to play. A presentation requires a structure and development. Your plan calls for analysis, for objectivity, and a focus on the task to be done. The simplest talk needs a beginning, a middle, and an end. Even a response to a question benefits from a structure.

Imagine your presentation as a piece of paper folded three times with your title written on the outside. Open once to form a larger piece; this represents the statement of your main event. A second unfolding offers space to restate your idea in a manner that is different in form but not content. This allows you to amplify and illustrate. The final unfolding permits you to reiterate your main event and press toward resolution, discuss verification, and bring your presentation to a close. The word *develop* comes from the Latin for unfolding. We infer that time needs to pass before ideas are accepted. People need to think about your thoughts, to weigh your arguments, and assess their consequences. This process is affected by the way that you present your idea and by the idea itself.

Your words will cause some reaction—perhaps negative. Classical rhetoric teaches us that every word evokes the idea of its opposite. Your task is to convince your listeners that you understand their ideas but that yours are better.

An idea that calls for change requires a carefully and effectively orchestrated oral presentation. This should dominate your thinking from the beginning. Everything that you do should lead inexorably to the moment when you present your idea to those with the power, the influence, and the resources to do something about it.

You must begin at the end. Ask yourself what you want from them: approval, applause, time, commitment, money, some other resources, blessing, or merely noninterference. The principal cause of failure in presentation is confusion of objective. When you don't know what you want, you can't ask for it. When you do not know where you want to go, as Alice learned in Wonderland, any path will do (see Figure 18).

Next, move from the objective to an idea of the structure of your plan, and a notion of what information you must convey. Then you have to figure how you will transmit that concept to other people so that they will act on it. Turning vision into action requires craft. Instinct is insufficient. How can you take what might be and make it into a picture that others can see? What can you say that will cause your idea to resonate in someone else's mind? What will give your thoughts the substance another person can grasp? Most managers spend most of the day talking, telling others what is important, listening for cues and clues. Others, engineers, for instance, may be more visually oriented, dependent on their charts and diagrams to help others see what they are trying to achieve as they attempt to clarify their picture of the world. Some people may grasp ideas in a kinesthetic way and will try to aid you in "getting a handle" on what they feel is important. Bandler and Grinder's recent work in linguistics suggests that astute managers will be alert to these nuances and will endeavor to match their presentations to their audience's perceptions of the world. If you are primarily a verbal person, you may want to develop stronger visual and kinesthetic skills. You will trap yourself if you use only your ears when you listen. As you add more strategies, you will be more flexible. For a group presentation, this means that you would explain your ideas in visual, auditory, *and* kinesthetic terms (see Figure 19).

Look at your audience. Success awaits those who understand and present their ideas from the viewpoint of the listener. This point needs to be written in bold and underlined whenever your idea involves:

Money
People
Property

Objective: _____

_____

_____

_____

What action could my listener or listeners
take that would let me know I have succeeded?

_____

_____

_____

_____

_____

_____

_____

Figure 18. Oral presentation: Preliminary Plan.

Changes in the way that things are done
Values and beliefs

Start from where they are. Build on your base of observation and
concentration skills. Think about their self-interest, their pride,
their anxieties. How do you know what their self-interest is? How

---

Listen to the words that other people use and try to
match the system that you hear. This can be visual,
auditory, or kinesthetic. With a group use all three
systems.

Word to listen for:

VISUAL
see
picture
lucid
murky
vivid
clear   AUDITORY
draw   hear
hazy   tell
envision   sound
               tune
KINESTHETIC   call
touch   dissonant
feel   ring
lead   harmony
lift
drag
grasp
heavy
guide
jar

Figure 19.   Communication systems.

do you know that you know? Every actor knows the necessity of playing to the opposition. Who are they? Who can join and help you in your enterprise? Who needs to be convinced? Who is likely to gain? Whose pride might be hurt?

You need to concentrate on a single objective. Save other objectives for another time. If you don't, you will clutter your message and fail to communicate what really matters. You want to present your vision in a way that stimulates the imagination of other people (see Figure 20).

People sometimes forget that an important goal in communication is to get ideas accepted and not merely recorded. They follow procedures, and send memorandum after memorandum with no result. In many organizations, the rules and the style seem to matter more than accomplishment.

If you have an idea worth telling, you have to be flexible in your approach and aware of what is happening around you. Someone says, "I've sent him four memos on how to improve productivity on this project, but he never bothers to answer." Another believes that because she has voiced her thoughts on new products she has been heard. As John Gardner put it, "Society develops elaborate defenses against new ideas, 'mind-forged

---

How will their self-interest be served
by my presentation?

What will it cost them? If anyone's pride or
purse be hurt, what can I do to mitigate the
situation? What problems will they have with my
ideas?

What do they know and believe? How is my idea
different from what they know and believe? How will
my ideas be understood in relation to that knowledge
and those beliefs?

What phrases, examples, figures, or charts would help
them to understand and act on what I will say.

Figure 20.   Audience analysis.

---

manacles' in William Blake's vivid phrase." Innovation is your key. Memoranda are seldom the answer. They are ineffective for mapping new territory.

As you plan, concentrate on the interests and values of your audience. Consider how your idea and your presentation connect with the values you hold in common with your audience. You can surmise, when you think about the interests of your audience, that those who have risen in the organization share the organization's values. Almost everyone, for example, wants to succeed and become a winner. We can surmise that the interests of your audience will include:

Pride

Productivity

Profit

Discipline

Optimism

Minimizing complaints

Thrift

Accomplishing goals

By and large, those doing the "big work" of the organization find their work important and challenging. It should not surprise you when they believe that free competition and individual effort are essential. Believing that success grows out of greater talent and devotion, they generally tend to believe that those who follow the rules get their just share of the rewards. In organizations today, performance, energy, and results count. If you want to achieve results, you need to be one of the team, part of the crowd. Each crowd, from Soho artists to computer programmers to Eastern Shore watermen to aeronautical engineers to Wall Street bankers, have their preferred dress, behavior, and style. There are lots of "crowds." In a complex society where there is interlocking activity, such implied cooperative behavior is preferred to rocking the boat. In some organizations, to be eccentric is to be one of the crowd. Consensus can smother mavericks. Visionary entrepreneurs lead the way in chemistry, astronautics, aeronautics, pharmaceuticals, bioengineering and manufacturing. For your audience, whether consensus builders or controversial risk-takers, excitement rests not in abrasive action, but in the tension of the race and the zest for winning. This is, of course, stereotypical thinking, but it provides you with a starting point when you are thinking about your audience and their interests.

As you work up your idea, look for ways to illustrate your presentation. Look for examples that give substance to your plan, look for words and phrases that tell your story. Your program must include plans for the meeting where you will present your main event. Always welcome the chance to make this presentation yourself. Resist any efforts to have someone else do it for you. Remember the legend of Priscilla Mullins and John Alden. Seek the opportunity yourself. If you have no choice, as in some hierarchal organizations, be sure to express your ideas in ways that both tell and show what matters. Endeavor to develop elegant models and diagrams that will aid your agent.

You must select the pieces, the fragments, that will enable others to see what you see, share your feelings of excitement, hear what you have to say. Your presentation can include illustrations and digressions that support the main event—but the main event must always stay in the front of your mind.

The most important mode of persuasion is *ethos*, the appearance of good will, good sense, and good moral character. Even more than appearance is needed. Believing in what you say is important. As Sophocles said, "The truth is always the strongest argument." If you tell yourself that it will be good for you if others believe that you believe, you should start all over. When you are devoting your energy to presenting a main event, it is worthwhile to find ways to express beliefs that make sense, that convey belief in what you are saying.

Without trust, you will go unheard. It doesn't matter how good your information is. Without trust, nothing else will matter. You need to build your credibility before you make a major presentation. Small successes and evidence of good citizenship build trust. If you have a reputation for hard work, honesty, and achievement, your major presentations will be received with more results than if you are unknown. Your plan for the main event could, especially if you are new in the organization, include a subplan to demonstrate your effectiveness: helping others, serving on a community fund or credit union committee, writing for an employee newsletter, volunteering for a vital but boring task, becoming visible in a positive way. A story is told of the proprietor of a new business who was advised to borrow money because repaying the loan would establish his reputation for reliability. Otherwise, no one would know.

The presentation itself requires:

Clarification of a single objective.

Focusing on what you want to achieve.

Illustrations and other elements to stimulate and appeal to the interests of your audience.

You need to keep this list in mind; otherwise, you may be tempted to include a few other worthwhile objectives or forget to let the audience know what you want from them. If you focus on your major elements, you will improve the chances that they will hear and act on what you say.

In planning, consider the problems of listening. If as a manager, you spend 60–80% of your time in meetings, you should spend most of that time listening. That is seldom the case. Perhaps we avoid listening because we are afraid that we may have our minds changed if we listen to other people's ideas. While we are talking, we can delude ourselves with the belief that we are in control. We may fear that if we really listen we will project ourselves and become lost in the other person's mind. Such a loss of control can be frightening and may explain why people fear the teaching of communism in the schools, why censorship gathers adherents, why some people are afraid of radical ideas. It is hard to believe that in 1939, the City Council of Cambridge, Massachusetts passed a resolution outlawing books and other printed materials containing the words Lenin and Leningrad. But now, more than forty years later, we are banning books in public libraries and schools.

Listening is difficult. This surprises people who have always assumed that talking is an active and listening a passive behavior.

Most of us wait impatiently while someone else is talking. We plan and even practice our responses while others speak, for we prefer our own ideas and opinions to those of others. Listening is a way for us to learn and gather new information. Only if you learn how to listen will you allow new ideas into your mind to connect with other thoughts and push aside outworn assumptions. Other people's views of the world help us to perfect our design, shape our thoughts into a view of reality which others can grasp and build with us. Listening requires courage and practice. Courage is necessary for leadership.

We can learn to listen better. A useful technique developed by Carl Rogers requires that each party restate to the speaker's satisfaction, what has just been said. That accomplished, you may present your own viewpoint. This means that you will have to concentrate on what the other person is saying. Sometimes, when I do this, I forget what I was going to say. That tells me something. Practicing this technique will make it available as a choice when you need it. You will better understand what the other person perceives to be relevant and important. It is tiring at first and unnerving to realize how poorly we usually listen and attend to others.

You will also be more effective. If you listen actively and consciously for even one hour a day at first, you will appreciate the new skills you are acquiring and will notice how careless you and others are. When you practice listening you can ask yourself:

How does my background block me from understanding other people's points of view?

How are my values different from theirs?

How am I trying to understand the other person's viewpoints and values?

To what extent am I rewarding or punishing others for agreeing or disagreeing with me?

You will enhance your effectiveness and your ability to understand yourself as well as others. If you not only learn to listen better but also show that you are paying attention, you will, in turn, encourage listening and efforts by others to understand you.

The skills that you acquire by listening to subordinates and colleagues will pay off in your presentation, especially whenever you must answer hostile questions that challenge your main event. Too often you can be sidetracked by a hostile question based on an erroneous assumption. We think that we have to answer a question just because someone has asked it. That is untrue; you have a choice. If you note the key words of the invalid assumption you can correct errors. What you don't hear can hurt. If you are going to counter what people say you've got to know what it is.

Distrust, distortion, and distraction can bar your success. The listener may be preoccupied or prejudiced. You may be too hurried. Selective inattention, ignorance, and obtuseness can spoil the attempt. You may have included too many ideas, or used words outside of your listener's experience. Your listeners may be too busy thinking of their reponses to hear what you have to say. You may be impatient; they may know too little or too much about the subject. They may just not give a damn.

Experience and experimental evidence tell us that it is easiest to communicate with those with whom we agree. We often simply do not hear those with whom we disagree. The more we believe we are right, the harder it is to change or examine our reasoning. Similarly, our listeners, rather than being persuaded of the value of our ideas, will try to convince us of their position.

People will often misunderstand us because they lack information about our ideas. The tendency in most communication is for us to underestimate people's intelligence and to overestimate their knowledge. The trick is to turn that around. We all know less than we think we know. What we learned in school, or even last week, is often obsolete, distorted, or untrue. There is so much around us: people, scenery, events, demands, that we delete information in order to simplify. Not only are we unaware of what we know, but we are also unaware of what we don't know. Norbert Wiener observed the paradox that the number of messages increases as a result of our technical communication capability, but more messages merely result in less information about fewer significant ideas. We live out T. S. Eliot's questions, "Where is the wisdom lost in knowledge? Where is the knowledge lost in information?"

We know enough to start. We know how to improve productivity, to make progress on the main event. But, despite our having the technology and the theories, things are not getting done. Innovations that could make the work place more humane as well as profitable fail to be implemented. Men and women, bent on accomplishment and finding it difficult to get a hearing, sense that their approach may be amiss.

One manager would walk in his director's office each morning and begin their conversation, "I have an idea to debate with you." He was shot down daily and began to dread the ordeal. He failed to see that he had been setting up a win—lose situation that was stacked against him. His boss had to win and did so everyday. When the manager learned to soften his opening gambit, he also began to persuade his director to consider new viewpoints.

What we often worry about is that others want something different from what we want. It may be that you have no idea of what they want. So many thoughts reverberate in your mind, most of them negative, that you can be overwhelmed. You need alternatives to either disregarding or being deluged by the data.

In dealing with a person with whom you expect to have negative experiences, information about what has worked in the past will give you choices. Who could help you? Ask other people for their experience, their knowledge of the other person. How has he or she reacted to similar experiences? Will the other person's pride be hurt? Will anybody be embarrassed? Will you?

How might your presentation create a negative impression? How does the other person feel about the subject? What are that person's self-interests? What is the worst thing that can happen? Will you die? Be fired? Be physically assaulted? The answer to the last three questions is probably "no." That helps to put the whole situation in a healthier perspective. Combine all your answers with your statement of objectives to create a total picture. If you have too much data, single out the most important facts. However, be certain that your approach is consistent with all of your information. If there is an underground spring on the site where you plan to build, you must say so. Otherwise, people may be surprised after the building is underway.

Your job is to prevent surprises. In most organizations you will be fired if you allow your superior to be surprised, especially if it is embarrassing. Your job is to make the boss look great. You can prevent unpleasantness if you remember that most of us like to be consulted and resent being told what to do. We like to be shown respect and allowed opportunity to be generous and human.

You may not get your way. Sometimes it won't matter how good your cause is or how well you prepare. What you want may not fit their plans. There may be extraneous matters that are totally outside of your control. They may just say "no." It is useful to set secondary goals: You can learn to understand the other person better and you can improve your ability to listen. Then, you always win something, even if they turn you down. Two out of three isn't bad.

Too much thought can lead to anxiety that stops action. Sometimes we tell people to think before they speak—as if that would solve their problem. Thinking is a good thing—it is wise to have your brain in gear before you open your mouth. Lots of people are paralyzed at the thought of communication and presentation. They would rather clean out the spider webs. This can be particularly true if you are going to propose a risky course, give a speech, negotiate for a raise, or ask for something costly. Anxious feelings churn in a tightening circle. "How can I get up the nerve to ask? What if I get turned down? What if they think that my idea is stupid? What if they think that I am stupid?" These free-floating fears can be quieted down if you concentrate on asking yourself: "What do I want to achieve and how am I going to go about it?" When you ask, "How can I solve a problem?" you are setting the scene for positive alternatives. There are no right or simple answers. A clear objective, a flexible plan, and sensitivity to what is going on right in front of you can help you get things done. If you are aware of the people you are talking to, you may detect that they are puzzled, or that something is unclear or outside their experience. When what you are doing doesn't work, do something else. Change your tone of voice or move your hands. Move to another position. Sometimes you might draw a picture.

You could use different words. There are lots of possibilities. Practice and effective performance can lead to elegant results, but you can create useful change without being elegant.

By planning and forecasting a conversation, you can substantially improve your chances of persuading someone to your point of view. If your idea is rejected, however, it is not you who has failed. A failure in program is just that, a failure in program. Your concept, your presentation, may have to go back to the drawing board. You may need to do more research, gather more supporters, clarify your objectives. The timing may be wrong or your idea may just have to be filed away with other future improvement projects.

Too much introspection creates clutter. This leads to inactivity and depression. Myths abound in organization about constraints and limitations. We are always hearing about what cannot be done. Inaction preserves and strengthens the myths that create clutter. This reduces the options that you and others should be considering. It is generally a good idea to push the limits until you are told to stop. As astronaut Kathleen Sullivan says, "It is easier to gain forgiveness than permission."

When people examine the discrepancies in communication that matter to them, they cite:

Not being able to get points across.
Inability to talk with others about anything important.
Misunderstanding what the boss wants.
Avoiding giving presentations.
Being told that behavior is threatening.
Being misunderstood.
Shyness in public.

These are important points and doing something about them could make a difference and have worthwhile consequences. It could be that training would be useful, especially in extemporaneous speech, in public speaking, or in giving presentations. There are extension courses in community colleges, in business schools, or workshops led by speech professionals. If your performance is less than desired but straining your ability, you might want to consider how often you communicate in public. If you do it regularly and are still having a problem, you need feedback on your specific behavior. Practice is important but, as Plato reminds us, "Practice gives us our best flute players and our worst flute players."

Like many other managers you may find that joining an organization like Toastmasters, which is devoted to helping people learn how to speak in public, will give you practice and feedback from colleagues struggling with the same problems. Videotape can help you study your performance and practice more effective behavior. Audiotape-recording is useful. A good friend or family member may be skilled at identifying specific behavior that hurts your presentation. If the problem is that you make presentations infrequently, you can gain experience through community, religious, or professional associations. When you do learn to make better presentations, you will brighten up and gain better control over your world. None of us enjoys bad experiences, failure, or humiliation in getting our ideas across.

Sometimes you meet unexpected hostility and anger. What matters then is your intent. Do you want to escalate the anger or resolve it? A manager of a major utility meets often with angry consumers. He makes a conscious effort to listen, absorb their hostile feelings, and offers few comments except to clarify his understanding of what they are saying. In less than half an hour at each meeting, someone in the group says, "We're being hard on him, let's listen to what he has to say." His restraint pays off. He remains in control of his own behavior and gains their attention and respect. What counts is what he does not say. When their anger is dissipated, he is able to firmly deny accusations of wrongdoing and credibly admit to errors. This enables him to bring the groups into serious discussion.

You can defuse insults, if you remain detached from them. Insults need not be accepted. You can acknowledge that some people might agree but that you believe something else. You could practice your fogging technique saying "Thank you for your concern," or "I appreciate your feedback." It is a good idea to practice these techniques in small matters, so that you will not be thrown off base in a major presentation. Staying in control requires discipline and practice.

Although some people deliberately put obstacles in your way or sabotage your efforts, most are too lazy for all that. They depend on inertia to stop or slow down other peoples' projects. Some people will seem to be working overtime at being difficult. If your story is worth telling you must be vigilant and ready for their attacks.

You are in trouble when another person believes that you think you are right. That person may just be cranky but possibly also feels assaulted by your ideas. People avoid getting hit. What you are striving for is "What is right?" not "Who is right?" Your task is to keep the focus on the issues, on the ideas necessary for an intelligent decision. It is useful to find ideas on which you both agree. This makes it easier for the other person to listen to you.

If you must present negative ideas, mention the positive ones first. Say: "The proposal is well-organized and well-stated but misses a few essential points." This statement leads your listener to infer that your judgment is pretty good. You are then able to focus on issues. It is useful to agree initially with the other person. Congressional debates provide us with a model. The gentlemen and gentleladies of the House and Senate first compliment one another on their eloquence and service to the nation. Only then do they criticize the legislation. This is not mere flattery: It works. By finding something good to say about your opponents, you are sharing their world and making it more likely that they will try to share yours.

Arguments can create clutter. Although they seldom solve problems, some people seek them for excitement, to release energy, and to relieve boredom. Their utility at work is questionable. When the noise level rises, it is hard for us to hear one another. It become impossible to organize and present material, to remain flexible. The din is too great. We become so anxious to get our points across that we fail to listen. As feelings escalate, we talk louder and repeat ourselves. Our goals forgotten, we adopt a new slogan: "Beat the enemy." We lose sight of the main event. Our effectiveness is impaired and, at worst, we find it difficult to work together. This can hurt our ability to get things done.

When disaster strikes, you may have no choice about making a presentation and little time for preparation. Take enough time to commit yourself to what is important for you to say. That commitment is a main event. If you are speaking for an organization, speak as that organization, not as yourself. This is one of those times when being accurate and being quoted accurately is more important than having your name spelled right. If there is a terrible question that you don't want to answer, they will ask it. Don't say "No comment" when you mean "I don't know," and don't say "I don't know" when you mean "No comment." If it's true, say "I have no other information at this time," or "It would be inappropriate and premature speculation on my part to answer that question. I haven't the facts." Remember that your total message counts. If you can be quoted out of context, you will be. It is difficult to keep control in volatile situations, but it is worth the effort (see Figure 21). If you are clear about your own convictions, your enthusiasm and opinions will add to your credibility.

Clarify objective and conviction.

Write down the main points to be covered.

Plan answers to tough questions.

Check and recheck on the data for answering difficult technical questions.

Plan simple statistics.

If pictures, models, or simple charts would be useful, bring them.

Assemble useful examples, quotations, and anecdotes.

Write out your opening sentence.

Plan acknowledgement of bias, errors, and inconsistencies.

Figure 21.   Preparing for confrontation.

You can disarm those who mistrust your stand if you say
"There are those who would say that I was biased but. . . ."
Humor is useful if appropriate. There are no simple and foolproof
answers. You will simply have to remain aware of what is going
on in front of you.

Confrontation is a double-edged sword. When you are caught
in a brawl, do what you can to make it a fair fight. Quiet indigna-
tion will often serve you best in an attack. If you can retain your
self-control, you may win on points. We feel bad when someone
else controls our contributions to a discussion. Keep in mind that
it is probably all right for you to say "I made a mistake, I was
wrong, I changed my mind." What sometimes happens is that
we say, "He made me angry," "It's their fault that I jumped to
that conclusion," "They infuriate me." When we assign responsibility to other people or other sources, we lose touch with our
feelings and give others control over us. That feels like losing.
The acts of others do not cause our emotions. Your emotions are a
response to what you see, hear, smell, feel, or touch. If, similarly,
you say "They have it in for us," or "They're against us," you are
practicing a kind of mind reading, claiming that you know the
thoughts or emotion of the other person. You may be accurate
when you say that someone is in a good or a bad mood, but you
are working on what you are picking up from the outside. You
may be wrong and simply responding to your own mood. This
can lead to trapping yourself in self-fulfilling prophecies like:
"We'll never get what we want from them." When you do this,
you lose your ability to experience the world directly. These
distortions are critical because they demonstrate ways that we let
clutter get in our way. Our presentations suffer when we fail to
stay in touch with our own feelings.

Some people seeing a gesture of rejection actually "hear" the
unspoken words "Go away." If someone yells and throws down
a piece of paper, we may "see" it thrown at the other person. If
we see a sneer on someone's face, we may feel bad. We hear a
scream and feel scared, we see blood and feel sick. This fuzzy
thinking is especially related to stress and underscores the need
for you to develop your sensory awareness in order to be more
effective. When several witnesses to a violent event describe

what happened, there will be sharp discrepancies. Details are omitted. Emotional responses distort and invent.

We see and experience events differently from everyone else. A meteorologist tracks the snowstorm and measures the snow's depth, the velocity of the wind, and the temperature. The artist may be drawn to the color and reflections of light, the shadows and shapes of objects covered by the snow. When I have a cold and would rather be in Barbados, I experience snow with revulsion. A skier responds with joy. The Eskimo has, some say, seventy words to describe different kinds of snow. You may know about "heavy," "wet," "powder," and "light" snow with big flakes or small. A native child on a Caribbean Island cannot grasp the concept when you try tell her. She has never been cold. There are no comparisons in her world. Ice cream and ice cubes are no help. Your perception is shaped by your experience, your geography, your history, your expectations, your needs, even your health and outlook at a given time.

Not surprisingly, when we have pleasant experiences, we react more favorably to people and events than we do when we are in a bad mood. In an experiment in which people received some kind of unexpected bonus, they were more likely to offer assistance to strangers than those who received nothing. The bonus was tiny—a dime planted for them to discover in a public telephone. This and similar studies seem to indicate, not surprisingly, that when people are in a good mood or have had positive experiences with others, they tend to accept one another better.

We all generally make the best choices available to us in our model of the world. Given appropriate resources, you can expand and change that model to accept other ideas. This also makes it possible for you to present your ideas better, so that they can be heard and accepted by others.

Some years back, a public relations manager was faced with hiring a young man with long hair as a secretary or doing without clerical help. He had never had a male secretary and did not like the idea. He figured that it would be bad for business. Although he also had strong negative feelings about the way young people were dressing and behaving, he felt that he had no choice. The young man proved to be an excellent secretary: a flawless typist, well organized, courteous, pleasant to work with and intelligent. The manager's old perceptions were no longer valid. He asked the personnel department for more long-haired male secretaries.

Each of us is constantly bargaining with reality, balancing what is inside of us with what we experience from the outside. You do not get your perceptions from what is out there alone. Your perceptions are filtered mysteriously through your nervous system. Adelbert Ames's work in optics and perception during the first half of the century demonstrated that perception comes from inside of us, that what we perceive is largely a function of previous experience, our assumptions, and our purposes. He studied how we deal with reality. His work showed Einstein, Whitehead, and Dewey, among others, that we are unlikely to alter perceptions unless we are frustrated in our efforts to act on them. Since each of us perceives the world uniquely, the process of being an effective social being is contingent upon our seeing the other's viewpoint. Thus, the meaning of perception is revealed in how it causes us to act. My reality is a separate experience from your reality. John Dewey and H. Cantril pointed out that what human beings are and what they make their environment into is a product of a mutually simultaneous, highly complex bargaining process between what is inside us and what is outside. We each perceive the world differently based on what we need and want to perceive, and on what our experience or intuition tells us will work. We are more likely, like the public relations manager, to change our perceptions when old ones no longer work. We do change our minds when new ideas offer opportunity for betterment. In particular, we change when:

Our self-interest is served.

Our experience is favorable and makes us open to new ideas.

We have not made a major issue about our opposition.

It is the inconsistencies in our value systems that make it possible for us to change our minds. If you have a very strong opinion on the defense system of the nation or abortion or the music of

Mahler, it is difficult for someone to influence you. However, if someone presents you with an idea or a solution to a problem about which you have no strong opinion, you can give it serious thought. Although you may vaguely favor lower local taxes, you may change your mind when someone makes a case for the value of a community swimming pool, if it would benefit you and your family.

None of us, however, will accept an idea if it does not fit our picture of reality. When you tell people something, they make something else of it that fits their map of reality, that is their own. It will not be exactly what you had in mind and tried to convey to them. Your listeners have their needs, their expectations, their history, their biases. They draw their own pictures. You are in trouble if you take for granted that someone understands what you are talking about. What they hear is the communication, not what you say. What they make of what you say is what matters. Your good intentions are irrelevant.

As listeners, we have to expand our map of reality. We cannot accept the ideas of others if we are rigid and closed to their perceptions. Michelangelo, Copernicus, the Wright brothers, Robert Goddard, Gerard Manley Hopkins, and countless other inventors, poets, and ordinary people experience the pain of trying to get new ideas accepted. Today, it is·hard to believe that concertgoers rioted at the premieres of Stravinsky's *Sacre du Printemps*, and Brahms's First Symphony. It is difficult to understand the furor over James Joyce's *Ulysses* or the Armory Art Show of 1913.

Recently, when watching the old Don Ameche film about Alexander Graham Bell on television, I wondered who the Bells are today, trying to sell ideas to nonbelievers. We seldom notice when we say: "We've always done it this way." Few of us see ourselves closing off from new experience as rigidity invisibly creeps up on us. Children and artists can teach us, but our society undervalues what they could contribute to our learning. Wisdom tells us that young people and artists—both with the manic streak of life—can keep us in touch with our senses. This acuity and conscious flexibility can help you to see, hear, and better grasp what is going on around you. There is a much larger reality that we cannot perceive, for each of us can only divide reality in two parts: our own and everything else.

This underscores the need to be flexible, to be aware of what is going on around us. Sometimes it can be funny, but only in retrospect, when we present an idea without being aware that people are ready to buy it. We have been so intent on what we are saying that we pay no attention to our listeners. Every salesperson I have ever known tells of delivering a "pitch" and missing cues that the customer was ready to buy. They all lost the sale. If you push on after you have struck oil you can be drowned in the gusher. In times of stress, and a presentation can be stressful, we are often blind to what is happening right in front of us. We lose sight of the alternatives. If you have planned for and practiced different possibilities and thought through how you might act in different situations, you are less likely to be rattled.

As in creative planning, your task in communication is to have many methods of approaching the situation. Recent studies of effective communicators indicate that in their presentations they integrate a wide range of approaches, demonstrate flexibility and a large store of useful fragments and tools. A style that enables you to develop sensory acuity may require you to use the right brain to be sensitive, receptive, cooperative, supportive, tentative, exploring, and intuitive, while you also use the left brain to be active, intellectual, competitive, objective, appropriately aggressive and task oriented. Combined, this enables you to both analyze and synthesize the situation, seeing it in an holistic fashion but being able to present your story in a structured, straightforward way.

What we have to say is made harder by the words themselves. Language is an invisible environment, a code, that profoundly affects how a society sees the world. Most of that expression is unconscious. The water is in the fish, and the fish is in the water. Our biases remain invisible to us. It is almost impossible for us to be conscious of the assumptions that control our culture. No matter how hard we try to understand one another's reality we remain essentially alone with our own map. We put our vision of reality into a code that we call language. No words, however, describe some kinds of experiences. Euphemisms obscure discomfort. Words mean different things to different people. Those to whom we speak uncode our code using their own code. Although we share some codes, we never really know anyone else's. What fools us is that we appear to speak the same language.

If we could but see through the eyes of others, what a leap that would make in our understanding. "Oh what gift the Giftee gie us/To see ourselves as ithers see us." Lacking that magic talent, we need to discipline ourselves to listen, to observe, to notice the words that people use, as well as their tone of voice, breathing, gestures, rate of speech, and posture. The more that you open yourself to the meanings that are in other people, the more you will generate and acquire new meaning yourself.

First impressions are important in oral communication. As soon as we perceive any facts, they will be sorted into some kind of meaningful whole. When we talk to anyone, the first words out of our mouths form an immediate impression in the other person's mind. You cannot know if it will be what you intended. In fact, you can be sure that it is different from what you had in mind.

The mind forms concepts so fast that even word order is important. For example, consider James, a cold person who is considered to be ambitious, hard working, and intelligent. Compare James to John, a warm person who is considered to be ambitious, hard working, and intelligent. Imagine these same descriptions for Duane who is black, Leonidas who is a short fat man, Karla who is an elegant blonde, Martha who is a New Yorker. Because our minds fall easily into stereotypes, you may react negatively or positively to the initial concept. This is the basis of much prejudice. You may have an adverse reaction to Leonidas sight unseen or to New Yorkers, or elegant blondes, or blacks. Some will see ambition as a positive attribute. Others believe that ambition is a bad thing.

You have a short time to make your first impression. It can last in people's minds. Another way of looking at this idea is to examine word order in a description. Because the concept is formed quickly, notice how the first word sets the pattern: intelligent, hard working, ambitious, skeptical, argumentative. Most managers tell me that such a description fits them. They say that they would hire someone with those characteristics. When I switch the order around: argumentative, skeptical, ambitious, hard working, intelligent, the picture is different, and they are hesitant. Your first sentence is your most important sentence. Often it is harder to write than the whole rest of the presentation.

Once you have that first sentence, you can design the rest of your presentation to get to the issues you want to discuss. If you study effective speakers at work on television and radio, you can note that they:

Use short, simple declarative sentences.

Give specific examples.

Quote authorities.

Use simple pictures and charts.

Use statistics that are easy to grasp.

When organizing material for your presentation, plan to state your goal early and tell them how you will move toward that goal. This will get attention. You want them to know that you are serious and clear about what you want them to do. More than one route leads to your goal. Assess the costs of each. The best solution may be too time-consuming, expensive, or politically unwise. The most probable idea may be a compromise. Don't lock yourself into a single approach. Outline each path but save the best and most probable for last.

Because we are impatient and because executive time is costly, you should get to the point quickly. The attention span of your listener is short, and use of technology may make it even shorter. On major television talk shows, a speaker may have less than two minutes to get an idea across. The eight-minute stories on Charles Kuralt's "Sunday Morning" were described by a critic as "leisurely." To discipline yourself, you could write your major message in eighty-five words. This would force you to get to the heart of the matter. If you average sixteen words to a sentence, that gives you about five sentences to tell your story and takes about ninety seconds. In all probability you will have more than ninety seconds, but don't count on it. If you have the time, you can enhance your message, demonstrate and illustrate your argument. Plan the aesthetics that will reinforce what you are saying. Use digressions and illustrations (see Figure 22).

Your presentation must be accurate, factual, and businesslike, but not boring. Use the opportunity to bring your ideas down to earth with anecdotes and apt analogies. This will flesh out your story. Anecdotes appeal to our common sense and imagination. Aesthetics adorn your main event and reinforce its truth. If possible, use humor. In job interviews, in particular, I've noted that laughter enables people to break down the glass walls that, often unconsciously, we build to protect ourselves from strangers. There is relaxation after laughter. During that time, the critical faculty is lowered. This is a good time to present a new idea. In his

---

Brief statement of major message:

_____

_____

_____

_____

Supporting ideas:
    Identify interests of audience
    Information on who, what, when,
    where, why, and how.
    Secondary but related ideas

To reinforce message:
    Examples
    Anecdotes
    Analogies
    Statistics
    Quotations

Figure 22.   Presentation.

---

first speech to Congress after the attempt on his life, President Reagan effectively told the story of a little boy who feared that the President would have to make his speech in his pajamas. His audience laughed, and the President launched into a serious discussion of his economic plan. It is hard to resist an idea that we hear after we laugh or cry.

Analogies are an important art form. They always contain basic untruths but they are invaluable in helping us grasp new ideas. You need to know the weak point in your own analogy. Perhaps you might point it out to your audience. Nevertheless, present your analogy with conviction. Analogy can help others to grasp as lively ideas that might otherwise appear arid.

Visual aids can be helpful. In some organizations, they are a way of life. Charts and films may be used. Viewgraphs help your audience to both hear and see your main ideas. Use large simple type. Ideally, a viewgraph should have no more than seventeen words of copy. This is difficult in organizations that are addicted to "nounisms." Sometimes titles such as the "functional redundant contingency configuration management division" add to the obfuscation. You would count such titles as one word, and do whatever you can to eliminate unnecessary wordiness. Pictures have an amazing ability to convey precise information however crudely drawn. The best viewgraphs I have ever seen were hand drawn by the executives who used them. They were fresh and telling. You can test your ideas in a number of forms to discover what works best. Strive for elegant simplicity.

If you are using visual tools to enhance your presentation, rehearse with them. With viewgraphs, it can be difficult to run from the podium to the opaque projector. You can use an opaque projector alone while you speak if the projector is right next to you. Take time to practice because the mechanical differences between machines can be maddening. You may want to put your notes on large cards in a looseleaf notebook. Large type is a good idea. Paper copies of your viewgraphs may serve as your notes. They can be illustrated with symbols to remind you, if necessary, to smile, look at your audience, or to lower your voice to emphasize a particular word.

For a large meeting, practice using audio or videotape. If the latter, take note of gestures, voice habits, verbal crutches, and jargon that detracts from what you are trying to say. Watch your total appearance. See that your eyes make contact with your imaginary audience. Note your breathing, your posture, your expressions. Studies show that we communicate our feelings 55% through facial expression, 38% by vocal expression, and only 7% by our verbal expression. You can never not communicate.

For a one-to-one meeting, when you practice, try role reversal. That is, give your presentation but reverse roles from time to time to gauge how the other person might react. Close the door to your office and practice sitting, moving, gesturing, and speaking as that person does. Managers who do this tell me they at first feel uncomfortable, but that it works. You often get insights into the other person's behavior. If you walk in their shoes, you will probably identify their tougher questions and be able to prepare your answers. Don't memorize what you are going to say. You may sound stilted and stale. Planning and practice can increase your control, eliminate worry, and help you be more relaxed.

As the moment approaches, so does stage fright. Your body feels threatened by what is going on but doesn't know the difference between a physical and mental attack. Your body only knows that you are in trouble. You may believe that you are. Stage fright is good if it makes you think better and stay alert. It is no fun if it comes on like seasickness. Many people fear public appearances and believe that they'll make fools of themselves. Some go so far as to believe that they will suffer a nausea attack while on stage. If you feel that bad, arrange for a bucket off stage and excuse yourself if necessary. Don't have a drink or take a tranquilizer or eat heavily. Being well-prepared is the best antidote. You may still be shaky but others will not notice.

With your presentation prepared, you can consider your environment and the ceremonies of presentation. Check the room, if possible, and do whatever you can to enhance its comfort. Arrive early to the meeting, talk with people, and introduce yourself to anyone you do not know. You are on stage all the time. This means that courtesy, consideration, and ease are essential.

A meeting concerning your main event needs to be controlled. You want to model productivity and effectiveness. Start on time to reward those who come early. When you distribute your agenda, indicate the termination time and the major issue under consideration. Plan a brisk opening and describe the format of the meeting. Don't delay in getting to your main event. Some people, when it seems appropriate, feel the need to put a few throwaway items at the head of the agenda. This can absorb opposition. Support and emphasize your principal points. Tell people what you are going to tell them, tell them, then tell them what you told them. With their interests in your mind, make your request of what you want them to do. If extraneous matters arise, suggest that they are good subjects for another meeting. Come to a clear, creative, and timely conclusion.

The people to whom you make your presentation have resources, access to what you need, and the ability to influence others to give you what you want. The way you present yourself can let others see that you are strong and know how to use resources yourself. Your job is to convince them you are competent and can do what you say you can do. They will not give anything valuable to someone who is weak. They will, however, share their power with those whose competence is apparent. Competence is power. If you are effective, those who support you will share in your accomplishment. It will serve their pride.

You want to be perceived as sensible, purposeful, and intelligent. You don't want to be seen as boring or foolish. This realization can help you to direct your thinking. If you are serious about bettering your communication skills, take a minute or two after any meeting to evaluate how well you presented your idea, responded to tough questions, listened and moved toward understanding the other person (see Figure 23).

By keeping your eye on your main event, you can avoid the trap of fighting for everything. Always let others win something. Save your energy for the important issues. Give away some points. Your self-interest can be served by letting the other person learn how important the main event is to you.

A woman met with her older brothers and sisters to divide the family possessions after their parents' deaths. She made up a list of some special family pieces that she wanted. There was one particularly fine Philadelphia highboy in her mother's room that held many special memories for her. It was also a very valuable piece of furniture. She also wanted some furniture for a guest room, a few favorite paintings, and her paternal grandmother's china. As the family "baby," she expected that her brothers and sisters would try their usual takeover techniques. She volunteered to type the inventory, and she carefully put the highboy in the middle. She was also careful to let her brothers and sisters win at least two major items right at the beginning of the negotiation. She made no claims, supported each one in turn and served as mediator. Having done so, she asked for their support in her request for the highboy. She went home with the highboy and with every other item on her list plus some that her sisters and brothers thought she should have.

She found a way to win her request. Being articulate is not the key. Articulate, powerless people are ignored. The key is being seen as having power. Power is sometimes found in the "chits" you can call in, whether for a highboy, a job, a raise, or support for a program. Power can be clout, but there are better solutions than intimidation. The ideal is for everyone to win something. In

Overall assessment of how it went.

What is going to happen as a result of the presentation?

Is that what I wanted to have happen?

What did I do that was most effective and helpful?

What do I want to do better next time?

What did the audience communicate to me?

What did I learn about myself, about them, about my subject, and about communication?

Figure 23.   Evaluation: Notes on presentation.

everyday life, as George Peabody teaches, "Power is the ability to do and get whatever it is that you want."

Effective communication requires that everyone involved be strong and appear strong. Many people, especially women and minorities, are perceived as nonmembers of the dominant group. Their requests are often unheard and undervalued. The problem appears to be that those who are in charge are reluctant to relinquish their dominance. It is not an attractive idea to think that the weak are the second sex, but if any of us are to be taken seriously, we must be seen as potent by those with whom we talk. Also, if we are to achieve, we have to be seen as achievers. To communicate a main event to *them*, you have to be seen as one of *them*.

Our ability to understand others, despite our continuing effort, seems to have superficial results. Pushing against our ignorance can be a harrowing process but it is rewarding to study what it is that differentiates *you* from *them*. Rosalind Russell once said that the most important thing she learned about acting was to listen.

By developing an awareness of how you and others communicate, you'll gain control, self direction, power. True mastery of communication is almost impossible. Your efforts at concentration, observation, and listening can allow you, not to manipulate, but to enter, ever so slightly, other people's worlds and to follow their leads. However, you must be alert, as R. G. H. Sui tells us, to "retain a healthy balance tinted with just that trace of paranoia that provides the tingling alertness so critical for vigilance." Fortunately, despite ineptitude and carelessness, people often do the right things, even if for the wrong reasons. You have to keep in mind that eloquence is not the object, nor applause, nor even clarity. What you say is not what counts. What counts is what you have them do.

Six

In Charge

BUILDING YOUR CAREER

Plans are worthless, planning is essential.
DWIGHT DAVID EISENHOWER

*The sins of our leaders will eventually
have their effect on us, too.*
JACQUELINE WEI MINTZ

Never crystalize.
ANAÏS NIN

Our best-managed organizations tell us that career management is essential. Most people who feel they have succeeded in their careers have planned, consciously set, and achieved important work and development goals. Studies by social scientists affirm that those who put effort into personal goal-setting report satisfaction with their work. They see a relationship between goal-setting and satisfaction. If you work for General Electric, IBM, or Exxon, half of your career-planning work has been done for you. However, no matter how well-intentioned your employer, you should never abdicate career planning to anyone else. With the best intentions in the world they can steer you wrong.

A recently fired senior executive had risen as the protege of a boss now discredited and now fired himself. Although the executive had been placed in higher and higher managerial roles, he was clearly not a leader. Formerly, he had built a solid career in sales based on his own desires and talent. When he ignored his own goals and let his boss plan his career, he ended up in an area where he could only fail. Today, he is the baffled victim of someone else's career plan.

Most organizations hold that career planning is important, but they take no action. You have to do it yourself. This can be difficult if you have little experience with career planning and have no idea where to begin. Most managers share this ignorance. Because we all work, all have careers, it seems as if we should know about career development. That is rarely the case. We are caught up in the daily work of draining the swamp and patching ourselves up after encounters with dragons. We forget to look ahead to see where we are going. Most of us fail to think about what we want to do. We seldom assess our preferences, study our strengths and weaknesses, or plan ways to build on those strengths.

The majority of managers give insufficient thought to

How careers develop.

How talents can be identified.

What opportunities and resources for development are available.

Career planning is everyone's job, but everybody's job becomes nobody's. In the best of all possible worlds, the chief executive officer sets the pace by careful attention to his or her own career and by developing others in the organization. When that is not happening, it is a mistake to sit around waiting. With Andrew Marvell, we hear "Time's winged chariot drawing near." You must assume that your development is your responsibility. Whereas this may be unusual in your organization, no one can say that you are behaving inappropriately.

Most people spend less time thinking about their careers than about choosing a house or selecting an automobile. The economics are staggering. Hundreds of thousands of dollars, even millions, are at stake. People just trust luck or seek an instant career program like the latest diet book. Self-development is one of those jobs that we are always putting off, to our own peril. Few recognize that career planning is a lifelong activity, a continuing responsibility.

Various studies report that more than half of all executives are unhappy in their work. Most do nothing but complain and dream of escape. They make no effort to change the situation. They sit in their wells staring at the walls. If people drop in, they make excuses for living as they do. Few try to climb out. It is depressing when people make so little effort to improve their lives. Most sincerely believe that they have no control over the situation. Even white rats in a maze remind us that when something is not working you must try another route.

You may never give serious thought to career planning unless you are fired. Both loss of employment and promotion push people into career planning. Threat motivates—as does enhanced self-esteem. If neither circumstance occurs, you have to motivate yourself. That's a problem if you are unsure of where to start and feel inhibited about serious career planning (see Figure 24).

With Peter Drucker, you may say, "I don't know what I want to be when I grow up." Only a few people decide at an early age what they want to do and pursue that objective without deviation. Those who find their calling at the age of ten tend to be doctors, farmers, pure mathematicians, ball players, dancers, composers, and concert pianists. Limited opportunities constrain us as does investment of time, energy, and money. Career crises face many teenagers who had planned to be artists and athletes. Two-thirds of those who apply fail to be accepted into medical school and must make radical changes in their lives before they are even graduated from college.

Most of us, however, have no clear vocation. We could have pursued several different careers and achieved considerable satisfaction from each. Some people with no visible calling are subject to paralyzing indecision. Others compulsively choose whatever is at hand. Mid-career crisis often relates to realistic regret about "choices" that just seemed to have happened at an earlier time. We have been brought up to do what was expected of us by parents, teachers, troop leaders, coaches, and friends. Most were trained to be what others wanted them to be. Now, they are puzzled, bemused, or angry at how they chose or were chosen for the work that they do.

Inexperience with planning.

Problems with decision making.

Lack of self-knowledge and rigidity in dealing with the environment.

Not knowing where to begin.

Limited knowledge of opportunity.

Excessive faith in the organization.

Belief that career planning is too time-consuming.

Negative self-image.

Anxiety and fear about failure.

Belief that individuals have no control over their careers.

Not knowing what works in career planning.

Belief that career planning is un-American.

Figure 24.   Hindrances to career planning.

Career planning seems to be an un-American activity. This may be a residue from years ago when the word planning connoted five-year plans, regimentation, and oppression. People hope that luck is the secret ingredient of success. They dream of being in the right place at the right time. Luck is, indeed, important, but these same managers would never go about acquisition or product development that way.

Managers who fail to take responsibility for their own careers place excessive faith in their organization. They persist in believing that if they work hard and do a good job they will be recognized and rewarded. If you believe that, you might as well believe in the tooth fairy. Serving splendidly is not rewarded. Serving splendidly is the reward. No evidence exists that management recognizes and promotes employees because of their excellent work. This never means that poor work is rewarded. Good work is expected. Poor work carries disproportionate penalties. If you do good work, they may let you stay.

Others say that they are too busy to think about the future. Such blind faith in tomorrow is unwise. It is another well. Burying yourself, cutting off family and friends, is unhealthy. You can paper your walls with your flow charts, hang your certificates of achievement, and tell everyone that you are too busy to plan ahead. You can just sit there.

Inaction breeds uncertainty. Uncertainty breeds inaction. Psychologists tell us that goal-setting can break that chain and provide a key to successful living. One reason that many people are unsuccessful is that they shift from activity to activity with no purpose, assuming naively that life will take care of itself. Those who report career satisfaction also report that they have consciously set goals, taken risks, and made their own luck. Those who drift and trust whatever fate brings them, include many who do not know what they want, or even what they like to do. They seem to want the whole pie and be unable to choose the piece that would be most satisfying.

That first step out of the well can be a giant one. For more than a week, a manager asked himself, "What do I want to do?" The words, "I hate what I'm doing, I want a different job" bubbled up. It can be easier to say what you don't want than to define what you do want. At first, he could only say what he disliked about where he worked. No one was on a first-name basis. Every procedure was documented. Every desk was like every other desk. Being on time was more important than achievement. Bells rang to announce the start and close of the coffee break, and everyone ate together in the staff dining room. Finally, he was able to say that he needed a less formal atmosphere and opportunity to be out-of-doors. Within a month he made a radical change, taking his skills to an informal social work agency. He is often at field centers that provide physical exercise programs. He performs a wide variety of tasks, including audits of accounts. He trains supervisors to prepare and monitor budgets. Although he has never worked harder or longer hours, he's never been happier. He says that the key was the time that he spent figuring out what was important to him. At first that seemed silly. Now he knows that his preferences are what matter.

Most of us also find it hard to understand that our desires count. It can be difficult to realize that you can have almost anything you want if you know what you want and don't ask for everything. You have to be willing to pay the price because no choice is free.

Some people with advantages fail to prosper; others with disadvantages succeed. Those who study careers observe that successful people recognize that confusion of objectives can be deadly. They put their energy into clarifying their goals, recording and analyzing what they do, and how certain situations make them feel. Much of this effort is tedious, but they do it because doing these things helps them achieve their goals.

Perhaps 60% of all career decisions, according to some executive recruiters, are based on chance. It ought to be worth more thought. People avoid learning about themselves. They stay in their wells. They say that they have no skills or that their abilities are unimportant. When they compare what they have achieved with what others are doing, they feel like failures. People want to have their careers improved, but not everyone wants to make the effort.

Although few people oppose career planning, most managers believe that it is a burden. They recognize that career planning enhances performance, but they also believe that it raises expectations and anxiety. Avoidance is common, perhaps because we'd be embarrassed if we announced a major goal and didn't achieve it. Failure is something we'd prefer not to talk about. We'd rather just hope for good luck. Insecurity explains a lot of overreaction to failure.

Although career planning can cause anxiety, unless you mobilize and arouse your expectations, you will have no new choices. Innovation can mean danger and frustration. Playing over your head makes you anxious, but being scared is one way to know that you are alive.

We are always discovering "last" taboos: money, sex, and, lately, power. Maybe the latest last taboo is failure. Although success can be bittersweet, winning is better than losing. We talk about success. We never talk about failing, about losing, about not achieving goals. We act as if failure were a disease that might contaminate us. We reject the idea that failure is simply a part of the human condition. When others win, we can even feel as if we have lost. Losing is an irrational absolute. Winning is relative, hard to define. You can be a winner when you finish a marathon, complete a major project, have a healthy baby, are named chief executive officer. The next day, with no warning, you can feel like a loser. Your confidence can be shaken if you are denied an opportunity that you wanted.

No one wants to fail or to be a failure. You want to succeed. You want to influence company policy, to be doing important work. You want the prestige that comes with building a reputation for achieving results. You'd like to lead a winning team. Success can mean the money for a French-style farmhouse near the beach. Success implies intention and commitment. Prosperity is, perhaps, the end result. Success is a process, never a fixed state. Willingness to work hard is necessary, but hard work is never enough. Many strive and fail. They never achieve their self-interest because, usually, they never figure out what their self-interest is.

The president of a good-sized company says that she has not succeeded because she is not president of a bigger company. The chairman of the board of an internationally known organization believes that he will never be a success because he sees no chance of a cabinet position or ambassadorship. A salesman earning almost half a million dollars a year feels that he missed his calling as a historian. The chairman of a prestigious department of astrophysics struggles with the bitterness of knowing that he will never win a Nobel prize. All four look successful to other people. Each privately speaks of failure.

The work place is a fertile ground for such fear. Worry that you will fail and be punished and rejected can rob you of self-confidence and inhibit your actions. Your fear can make you more fearful. It is a vicious cycle. If you act fearful, you will be cautious and become unable to act. This will, in turn, make you feel worse. Fear can lead you to hate yourself for your inaction. Your energy drained, you find yourself unable to work hard or concentrate on your objectives. This will prevent you from achieving goals. It is no fun at all.

These feelings at work are compounded if you have been unable to achieve other personal and family satisfactions. Sophocles wisely said that we should count no man lucky until the day that he dies.

We fear that we will never have the opportunity to develop and demonstrate our ability. Rather than deal straightforwardly with what we want and are willing to strive for, we drift through our days as if we could postpone the future. We wait for the chance to do things the next time, someday, tomorrow. As Lewis Carroll put, "Next time is now."

Many hesitate about career planning because they don't know where to start, what works, and what the benefits are. The field of career development is relatively new. Of the little research done, most is limited in scope and too conservative to be useful. Practitioners are jealous of their own methods. Some even claim that they alone have the answer, but despite all claims and counter-claims the process of career planning consists of only two parts: your preferences and your resources. The major question to ask yourself is: "What do I really want to do?" To answer, you need to look at what you have enjoyed, what accomplishments have been meaningful to you, what rewards you want, what abilities and talents you have. This can be a surprising approach if you have thought that careers and jobs start with the question "What's out there?" That reality is less relevant than the inner reality of your preferences and your resources.

You should work at figuring this out. "What do you want to do?" is a question that you could answer if your life depended on it. It does. It is all right if you don't have an answer now. What is important is to keep working at it. If your answer is a vague picture, trying to be clear will help. If brief, unrelated phrases resonate in your mind, attempt to listen to them. They may be important clues. Perhaps your feelings will come to the surface and enable you to grasp your idea of the future. Your task is to clarify what you want—delineate the goals you want to achieve.

Resources are the other part of the career process. You need to assess whatever would enable you to achieve your goals. If you picture those resources in your mind, you can see how you can draw on them to achieve your vision. You might listen to the words that tell you about your strengths, your experience, knowledge, and skills. You may need information about careers. People, too, are resources. They can listen to your ideas, tell you about new careers, advise and help you to achieve your goals. Writing down thoughts of how you can use your resources may help you to expand your ideas of what your resources are and to focus on those which are most important.

The process of career planning in self-help books, courses, workshops, and individual advising is merely geared to bring together your preferences and the resources that can move you toward their achievement. This synthesis and the actions that follow are the basis of all career programs. A kind of synergism results. Your odds of achieving success go up when you have a clear picture of what you want (see Figure 25).

To identify your preferences, you must first expand your view: review experiences, knowledge, achievements, and skills to see what you prefer. Then you must focus on what you most enjoy and want to do. The emphasis should be on action. What do you want to do?—the only valid question of career planning—can be answered by no one but you. If you say that you want to lead the company or to farm, the only response that anyone else can give you is "Why not?" It is up to you. You may of course have many responsibilities to consider and aptitudes to weigh. Risk is a factor. Nonetheless, they are your responsibilities, aptitudes, and risks.

If you find that the question is difficult, your feelings are shared by others. When I ask managers what they really want to do, most merely mumble that they want to be executives, to have authority and responsibility, or to be happy. Those are not answers to the question, "What do you want to do?" You can't "do" authority. You can't "do" executive. Most of us answer this way because we never give serious thought to what we do want.

You may believe that you have no opportunities. You could have closed off choices without knowing it. Some of us even prevent ourselves from liking our jobs by not finding out what we do like. You may discover that your job comes close to being what you want. Perhaps what you are doing expresses real needs of the organization, involves appropriate risk-taking, requires judgment, and encourages excellence and self-management.

Should your answers show that you are satisfied with what you are doing, your task is to determine how you want to grow,

---

Basic principles:
  Expand and focus.

  Synthesize your preferences and resources.

Basic steps:
  Analyze and synthesize knowledge,
  experience, talents, and skills.

  Explore and focus on opportunities within
  and outside the organization.

  Build a network of allies.

  Set and write down goals based on preferred
  strengths.

  Take action.

Figure 25. Career process.

---

and what you want to learn so that you can continue the process. This is how you prevent obsolescence. You need to be in touch with change and brave enough to try out what you are learning.

You could ask yourself questions about what is important to you (see Figure 26). If you write down what you like and dislike, you will force yourself to be exact about your preferences. I find that this enables me to look for important differences between what exists in my work and what really matters to me.

What is really important to me?

What achievements have mattered to me?

What were the rewards of those achievements?

What are my strengths, preferences, shortcomings, and resources?

How do my preferences connect with the main themes of the organization?

What do I like about what I am doing now?

What don't I like about what I am doing now?

What do I really want to do?

Figure 26. Career planning questions.

A manager often looks at someone else's job and says, "I could do that." That may be. Other people may be unaware of what you can do. If a particular job attracts you, ask yourself "What have I done lately that emphasizes my competency?" For example, should you be interviewed for an executive position, you might be asked to describe your accomplishments and what was important about them. You might describe how you developed a major project, set up a new organization, solved an unusual problem in recruitment, or monitored a program that resulted in large savings. You need to think very specifically about experiences in which you defined and established policy and integrated programs within the larger framework of the organization. Writing down your answers and examples from your experience and education can tell you how you can communicate your ability to others. It can also tell you of experience and education that you need for further success.

You might read your boss's position description and look for what does and does not attract you about it. Should you want to do that work, you can list what you need to learn to do. You should talk with someone who knows your work and the job to which you aspire. You may benefit from coaching and advice, particularly if you receive little feedback on your work. Often we believe that we are doing better than we are. Unfortunately, no one seems to care. Finding out is up to you. If you ask people what you do well, you may be surprised at what they tell you.

One woman found that others admired her warmth and skills with people but did not recognize her organizational ability. She made a point of volunteering and seeking opportunity to demonstrate this talent. The organization benefited, and she achieved the recognition she wanted.

If you tell others, in specific detail, about how and where they are effective, they may tell you how you are doing. Your objective in career planning is to build on your strengths. To do that, you need to know what your talents are. Ask those whose opinion you value what you might do to improve your performance.

You can verify your self-examination with people who know you in a variety of contexts. Their best contribution can be in evaluating and rating your strengths. These opinions can sharpen your analysis and tell you how well you know yourself.

You will want to look at what you want to be doing this year, next year, in five years, ten, twenty. How important to you are money, power, intellectual pursuit, security, recreation, family, friends, contribution to society? Few of us can turn recreational interests into big money, but some do. If you aim for the role of executive, you'll have little time for family and friends. You might as well be your own person when you set objectives. You'll never do well as anyone else.

In your world, it may be strange to be a scientist, a door-to-door salesman, a business leader, a politician. It is important for you to determine what you want to do and recognize that it may differ from what others expect of you.

An Ivy League graduate, who had become an insurance executive, changed careers five times seeking some sort of satisfaction. He hated every job and finally sold his agency. Career counselors thought he didn't want to work. One day when he was at home, a door-to-door salesman called and sold him some brushes. A few days later they met, by chance, at the village coffee shop. The former insurance man listened to the other man's story and felt attracted to the work. Immediately, he called the company and persuaded them to assign him to a territory. What appeals to him is that he goes someplace different every day. He is constantly meeting new people. He had hated the commuting routine to the office; moreover, he sets goals every day and achieves them. He needs that challenge. His old friends and classmates were surprised, but are pleased at the way his work has revived him. He is earning more money all the time and having a wonderful time.

Few make such a radical change. There is much that you could do right where you are. The most practical way for you to work seriously on your own development is to include career development in your work plans. If you do not believe that your self-development is part of your work, no one else will suggest that it is. If, however, you present a rational plan to foster your own development, others will accept it as part of your job. You could look for ways that your life could be enriched. Most managers are unaware of their ability to influence their own careers. Dependent on the organization, they often make no changes in their work or lives because they are waiting for someone else to do it.

Every six months, you could schedule a career checkup, preferably with a wise adviser—your spouse, supervisor, a higher level manager in another department, a colleague, a career advisor. In preparation for this meeting, it is useful to get away from the work place. One executive goes twice a year for a weekend alone at the beach. He takes along a copy of his position description to see if it is what he is doing. He makes a habit of taking home a copy of his accomplishments every month—presentations, pertinent reports, sales records. At his review, he looks at those achievements and assesses how he feels about them. His goal is to get in touch with what he wants to do. He endeavors to clarify his picture of what he wants the future to be and to put into words how he wants to proceed. His experience confirms how difficult it is to put in practice that ancient admonition: "Know thyself." He watches his wants and needs change and by studying his past and being alert to the present, he keeps discovering clues for the future. Another manager reviews goals monthly. Someone else uses the New Year's break for serious assessment of life goals. Another reviews her assets and plans when she does her income tax.

You cannot do everything, but you can do more. Practical considerations and other people's priorities intrude. If you stay in charge of your own development, you can work through and around a lot of impediments. Many people with no money, heavy responsibility, and handicaps of age, race, sex, and physical disability have refused to succumb to facing the facts. They refuse to hear those who insist that it is impossible for them to succeed. Using the principle of eliminating clutter and by scheduling blocks of time for important tasks, they carve out time regularly to focus their ideas on the future. They note habits they want to change. They look for actions to initiate. They enlarge their network of friends and colleagues and work to shape where they are going.

The value of career planning lies not in the plan but in the effort involved. In forcing ourselves to think through the factors that shape our lives, we can plan our careers rather than allow our careers to plan us. If for some reason, the plan has to be reworked, it is no matter. The planning skills have been learned. They are useful in other planning activities. The act of planning itself generates nerve, energy, and growth.

Either you are growing or you are dying, shrinking into obsolescence. Look around. There are great old people and terrible old people. You have no other choice. If you want to be a great old man or a great old woman, you should begin now. You can't begin when you retire. You need to find situations that stimulate and stretch your skills. High performance comes from concentrating on achieving goals, building successes, and focusing on the process. The task, as always, is to expand your choices and to focus on what matters. You will need to gather more information, weigh choices, concentrate. You may want to try something new, do better at something old, continue in your present course but add resources to your effort. That is what decision making is all about.

Decision making can be a pain. Even people who are usually decisive can have problems with certain decisions: hiring an employee, taking on a new program, changing the direction of a project. If employees complain about anything in their managers, it is that they are indecisive. We connect decision making with authority. We imagine those in charge as self-confident, assured, and decisive. Assertive, even aggressive people, however, sometimes hesitate about going in this direction or that. Not all of the time, but the tendency may be there.

People who are perfectionists can have special problems with decisions. They never want to settle for second-best. They want to make the ideal decision, have the perfect career, choose the best piece of pie. Although such standards are unrealistic, they cause highly regarded decision makers to experience anxiety and doubt, especially about career planning.

When you have trouble with a decision, it may be that you are unaware of something interfering with your ability to make a choice. One manager, unhappy about his work, talks incessantly about going to law school at night or looking for a new job. He has made no effort in either direction. While he tries to make up his mind, he remains in a job that he dislikes, hesitating over more and more decisions. He can no longer decide even what to pack for a business trip. He is beginning to wonder if he is uncomfortable about leaving the familiarity of his office and company.

Sometimes there are too many choices, too much opportunity. You can yearn for an earlier, simpler time with a short list of limited career possibilities like "doctor, lawyer, merchant, chief." You have thousands of choices. You can work anywhere in the country, around the world, under the sea, and even in space. We are the first society in history in which you can earn a living doing just about anything. People work making kites in Martha's Vineyard. They conduct walking tours in Annapolis, run worm farms in Arizona, catch tropical fish in Florida. They teach people to hang glide. Others write investor newsletters, install security systems, do time-lapse photography, test wine, run fast-food restaurants, serve as arbitrators, peer into electron microscopes, and build robots. It can be too much. Choice can be a burden. We are not surprised when people become overwhelmed and turn to career advisors to say, "Decide for me. Give me a career."

Perhaps you suspect that your career and interests have taken off in different directions. Psychological testing by a counseling firm may help you figure out how far you are from where you want to be. Testing can merely confirm what you know. Since these services can cost hundreds and even thousands of dollars, this can be expensive self-confirmation. Testing and advising can be useful when you are plagued by indecision, have no idea of what you want, or know what you prefer but can't figure out what to do about it.

Decisions often require giving up one thing to obtain something else. You may have to compromise, and give up your present security and habits for the insecurity of a new place, meeting new people, and learning new skills. A manager worried that by making a choice now, he will lose the freedom to take other opportunities that may come along in the future. People like that often feel trapped as soon as they choose anything. The reality is that few decisions are cast in concrete. If you select a course of action that goes nowhere, you can turn in another direction. If you take a job that is wrong, you can quit.

When you stop being afraid of making a mistake, you are more likely to recognize when things are going wrong. Alert to what is happening around you, you will be likely to change direction in time to prevent disaster. Your self-awareness and sense of identity can make decisions easier. If you know what you like and what you want, a lot of choices are automatic. That alone saves you time and energy.

The paradox, of course, is that fast decisions are never necessarily best. A manager in a small manufacturing firm decides with breathtaking speed but makes bad choices. She is unable to tolerate an unmade decision and acts impulsively when she should be exploring the situation. If, however, she deliberated slowly, she might waste her time and energy and do no better.

Agonizing for a prolonged period is no answer. Worry does not, necessarily, enhance the quality of the decision.

A famous professor of organization and operations research was invited to join another prestigious university three thousand miles away. His fame rested in part on a decision tree that he had developed. He was torn over the opportunity. The offer was attractive—a much higher salary, a new computer facility and laboratory, and the family's favorite sports nearby. It sounded like a wonderful adventure. He and his family, however, loved the university and the town in which they lived. They enjoyed the two-hundred-year-old home which they had restored themselves. Other family members and close friends lived nearby, the children were happy in school, and his wife had a job that was important to all of them as well as to the community. He agonized for weeks while his colleagues chided him for his indecision. They suggested that he use his computer to solve his problem. "Oh no," he said, "It is too important."

While there are reasons for decisions to cause us trouble, we seldom have to worry about them. Our need for parental love and approval, and our feelings about authority may be the causes, but we can still do something about improving our decision-making skills.

If you have problems in career planning—deciding what you like and want to do—you may have problems with other decisions. There are some pragmatic steps which may help you make better decisions.

You can start by writing down your choices and weighing their merits and disadvantages. Be sure that you have enough choices. Two is probably too few. Other people may be able to suggest other alternatives for you. However, if you have more than seven choices, you need to rank and narrow your list. You can ask yourself the worst thing that will happen should you choose any of your alternatives. You could pretend that you have decided. In your mind play the roles involved in accepting the new job, taking flying lessons, or moving to a new city. How does it feel? Set a deadline for yourself. Often you have a hard time making a decision because no choice is significantly better than the other. It is important just to make the decision. Only rarely will your commitment be permanent (see Figure 27). If all else fails, listen to your stomach.

Be sure that you have enough but not too many choices. Three to seven is about the right number.

Write down the good and bad points about each choice.

Ask for each choice, "What is the best and the worst thing that will happen if I make this choice?"

Set a deadline.

Listen to your stomach.

Pretend that you have decided.

Try it.

Figure 27.   Making a decision.

Indecision can produce unplanned consequences. Albert Camus said that not to decide is to decide. If you want to make a change in your career but do nothing, what happens? You take no steps, and time passes. Your decision is made by default.

If you decide by not deciding, ask yourself what is likely to happen. Is that what you want? If not, it is up to you to do something, take charge of your future. If you cannot deal with the situation, you might want to consult a career advisor or counselor.

Sometimes no decision is apparent. If you have been promoted by advancing in a specialty, like legal or personnel work, are at the top of your ladder, or have been catapulted into a position in an untraditional manner, you may see no opportunity ahead. A program analyst successfully served as acting director upon the director's sudden death. He not only maintained the programs effectively but also initiated the planning for a series of complex new projects. His ability was obvious, but the other directors had all come up through line management in the field. Despite his success as a manager in the corporate offices, without that experience he was considered ineligible for promotion to director. Realizing this, he proposed several alternative plans to his management, including a temporary lateral assignment to a regional office. They agreed that this would enable him to close the gap in his experience. He also made a point of arranging participation in the company's advanced management education program. His goal was to ensure his being perceived as a manager.

If others see you as a specialist, particularly a staff specialist, you must make the effort to gain broad experience. In large organizations you can get wide exposure only if you take the initiative. The organization will tend to cram you into a narrow niche. It is your job to aim for the bigger picture.

To be an effective executive, you must squarely reject the notion that you are a professional lawyer, scientist, writer, personnel officer, engineer, or salesperson. That can be painful. You have spent time and effort establishing yourself professionally. Your identity, your ego, and your prestige are based on your professional reputation. It is difficult to give that up, but there may be too few hours in the day for you to be a top expert in your field *and* a management leader. The choice is yours. If you would lead, your task is to move as rapidly as possible through several major functions—production, sales, operations, finance—to gain a broad picture of the work.

The basic way to learn to be a leader is to lead. That experience can be enhanced if it is regularly examined in a serious executive education program. Numerous universities, community colleges, and management-association courses can help you integrate theory and practice. A rigorous self-directed reading program can augment formal training.

If you have been stereotyped in a profession, you could earn an advanced degree in business administration. You can expect no guarantees. You will have to show them how you can apply this knowledge. Every large organization has several people with MBA's who are doing business in the same old way. It is what you do with your education and training that matters.

Your effectiveness requires that you understand the dependence inherent in your work. Although no profession is truly independent, some do emphasize individual effort. We sometimes joke cynically about teamwork in organizations, but it is important. Management has almost no room for independence. This doesn't mean that you conform. It does mean that you need to work effectively with individuals and with interdependent systems.

You may have five or six people reporting directly to you. They in turn have ten or a hundred subordinates. You also have to rely on the services and cooperation of a hundred other people in other divisions to get your projects done. They may be affected by hundreds more within and outside the organization. When they hold up your work, you have to move them, too. Their rules and procedures can stop your projects. It seems, sometimes, as if people stay up nights inventing obstacles.

You may have to find new ways to enlist the cooperation of those outside your organization. You will spend a large part of your day getting people to work with you, gathering information, dealing with delays, working out compromises. You never can just sit back and oversee the work.

It's your job to understand how the organization works. That's frustrating because nothing remains the same. The characters enter and exit, the scenery refuses to stand still. In fact, every change changes everything. Your career planning needs to address your ability to stop trouble and to accurately gauge when things are going well. Maintaining good relations and gaining the cooperation of the uncooperative are part of the challenge. You have to work with people who have other priorities and are busy with their own projects. Some individuals are incapable of helping you. Others have values and goals that are in direct conflict with yours. Gaining their cooperation or, at least, preventing their interference means that you must be looking for innovative and effective ways of working with them. You can seldom delegate this sort of activity. It takes time, skill, and prolonged effort. This is another argument for delegating predictable and routine activities.

When resources are scarce, cooperation seems impossible. Nonetheless, effective executives are the ones who understand that what matters is the total organization, not just their division. In a complex society, rocking the boat is ineffective. To get the oars clicking together, you have to match your stroke to your colleague's, and be certain that you are all headed in the same direction. You add or change your activities so that you interact more with others whose cooperation you need. It is a good sign when your support or advice is sought. If the signs are poor, your planning can address ways you can improve your ability to influence the system.

The more you know about your organization, the more effective you can be. You might ask yourself if you know how to work with contractors, check a client out with Dunn and Bradstreet, present a proposal, schedule production, settle a grievance, defend a budget, work with graphics, printing, and purchasing. You should make it your job to know how and where things get done so that you can do them faster and better than others. Information is power. So is competence. Once you know how to do these jobs, train a subordinate to do them. Otherwise people will depend upon you to make things work. You may feel flattered as a result, but that is not the main event. A reputation for cleverness, as Alice B. Toklas observed, is cheaply acquired and dearly maintained. What does matter is that you know the workings of the organization and who can help you in an emergency. You can achieve almost anything in a complex system but you may be blocked many times and have to use a number of approaches. Your time and energy are finite and require conservation.

A manager who wanted to be more involved in the allocation of resources proposed an interdepartmental budget assignment in her yearly performance plan. Continuing problems with the comptroller's office had hampered her group's work. She pointed out that her division would acquire, as a result of the joint budget assignment, better information and improved relations with the other division. This was not only true but appealed to her director's self-interest. She proposed training her subordinates to take over certain routine functions. Their training was also incorporated into her plan. The assignment called for her to participate in budget reviews of other departments. She was able to help with several rather delicate problems that had been costly in time and money. Her experience broadened her viewpoint and caused other people to know and notice her.

Being noticed is a major factor in your career development. You should look around to see what you can do. Some managers report the value of volunteering to organize the community fund drive or working on the company picnic. One manager noted that his career was advanced by his successful management of the corporation's basketball team.

After talent comes visibility. Making yourself known is absolutely essential. You have to devote time and effort to being noticed. This can include:

Getting your ideas in print.

Making speeches.

Serving for a brief time in local, state, or federal government.

Leading an in-house training program.

Participating in and leading meetings.

Some managers just concentrate on looking good. In meetings, for example, they demonstrate that they are well-prepared by asking searching questions and delivering artful, impromptu speeches.

You may plan, work, and hope for a promotion. In most organizations no one knows what the promotion process is. Whatever it is, it is bound to be different from what the organization says it is. Nowhere is policy administered uniformly. Although doing an outstanding job is necessary, doing an outstanding job will never assure you consideration for promotion. No one knows what else to do. "I've done a lot," someone said to me, "but what's enough?"

Rumors abound in organizations about how people get ahead. They say that you have to have gone to Harvard or the state college, that you must hold an advanced engineering degree, have field or headquarters experience, been to a management program at Stanford, or be an Episcopalian or Italian or play golf or have been raised in a small midwestern town. These rumors are false and true. No matter what you do or are, you may never be considered for an important job. You can be overwhelmed trying to figure out why. The probability is that whatever you believe is true about promotion in your organization is untrue. Those who make those decisions do not know what they want until they see it. They often choose the familiar because they are comfortable with what they know. They do know that they want a winner. If a better choice is placed before them, they may choose that which is less familiar. Your job, then, is to be perceived as a winner.

You will have to use everything. If you went to the company college or play the company sport, of course, that can be important. There are, however, many routes to success.

You will need current, complete, and reliable facts. Information is your lifeblood. Most managers appear to be prisoners in their offices, blind to what is going on down the corridor, in the next buildings, in the field centers, or at headquarters. If you have a good picture of your organization, you have a clear advantage over most managers.

If no matter what you do, you are certain that neither promotion nor improvement of your job situation is likely, you need to consider what other choices are possible. Should you be totally blocked by a superior who is not moving or dislikes you, you should do something (see Figure 28). Move, but don't run whenever you face trouble. Others may perceive you as making progress. If you are relatively happy, staying where you are could, in time, work to your advantage. You may benefit from advice of colleagues and other friends.

Should you feel really discouraged and dissatisfied, advance with caution. The literature is full of stories of people who quit jobs as advertising executives to run charming inns on the Maine coast, people who left major accounting firms to become comptrollers of small country colleges or resigned as sales managers of major manufacturing firms to become potters in California. Some people go from bad to worse. They may tell you that someone with your talent and experience will have no trouble finding a job. They lie. People jump into unemployment as if job offers would cushion the fall. Rarely do people find that career transition is easy. Our employment system is unfair, elitist, rigid, inefficient, and ineffective. It is not surprising that people talk of "the unemployment office," not "the employment service." There is no employment system.

Instead, thousands of dysfunctional systems allow thousands of jobs to remain unfilled while thousands of talented people strain to be employed. Those attempting to jump out of one career box into another usually get hurt. Before taking such a leap, you need to look around, expand and focus on your preferred skills and choices, and on the people who can help you make the change (see Figure 29). Whenever possible, you should avoid bridge burning. People turn up again and again in the most unexpected places. At the least, you may want a reference.

Quitting is, at times, the only answer, but it could be easier to redesign a job where you are. Your understanding of the new

---

Discover the cause of blockage.

Get more data and build a better case.

Consult with others.

Talk with your boss.

Continue to do excellent work.

Develop and try an alternate plan.

Take care of your health.

Build small successes.

Hang in there.

If the situation proves to be unsalvageable, move on.

Punt, and accept the lesson learned.

Don't panic.

Figure 28.   What to do when blocked.

experiences that you want and the problems and mission of the organization can help you show others where and how you could make a better contribution at work. From this you can plan a blueprint that could enable both you and the organization to measure the results. If you wait for permission to grow, you will continue to feel trapped and ill-used.

Should you, however, see a position that you want, swift action is the answer. Run, don't walk. An employee told the training manager of a large manufacturing company that she would like to work for her if there was an opening. Within a few months, during a reorganization, the manager was asked to add

Research preferences, assess experience, abilities, and knowledge.

Use the library to research career fields, associations, professional organizations, communities, employers, resume writing, job hunting.

Decide what is important.

Join and take an active role in professional organizations and associations.

Continue to help other people.

Clarify objectives.

Brush up on career and job hunting skills such as writing resumes and interviewing.

Interview people for information:
Geographical area.
Industry or field.
Specific organization.

Seek people who can:
Provide information.
Assist with assessment.
Refer to jobs or hire.

Figure 29.   Making a career switch.

another function and absorb one of two employees. One was the one who had earlier spoken to her. She considered the employee's organizational skills, her knowledge of the company, and interest in training and arranged the transfer. Some time later, the other employee told someone that he, too, would have liked to have joined the training staff. From this, he learned the importance of letting others know what he prefers and does well. He learned to make his circle of friends and advisors bigger and began to take a firm position on his own progress.

You can almost never aim for a particular future or find consistent historical patterns. You need to work through and around organizational realities. The paradox is that, whereas loyalty to the organization is necessary, you must also keep your own goals in mind. Essentially, you work for yourself. This sounds disloyal to the organization, but it means being loyal to yourself. To any work place, you are a hired hand. This is true for managers, management interns, supervisors, presidents, everyone. Most of us would never think of leaving the company without giving two weeks notice. Organizations seldom hesitate to ask people to leave the moment that they fire them. Naivete is fatal. The task, the main event, is to find opportunities, make the greatest contribution and receive personal satisfaction and rewards.

Planning your career is like catching a butterfly or holding a handful of water. If you grab tightly, see what happens. You may not get the promotion. The job that would allow you to shine may be given to someone else. Overnight, the place where you work can no longer be a good place for you to work. A larger company may take over and have no appreciation for your talent. They can hire a new boss who is venal and stupid. They can adopt new objectives which are at odds with your own values. Every change changes everything. Despite any sense of obligation, your task is to keep your loyalties straight.

Sometimes when life goes wrong, it is easier to adjust to living in the well than to climb out again. It is never easy to change habits, to analyze unproductive behavior, and to establish ways of working in a more effective way.

When disasters strike, your understanding of the planning process will help you make sensible and flexible decisions.

One young woman's career plan included attending a particular college. Although she was class valedictorian, president of her senior class, and had exceptionally high scholastic aptitude scores she was not admitted. Every year dozens of people are rejected by the Yale Law School even though they have straight A averages, and perfect scores on the law school entrance tests. The father of a sixteen-year-old has planned his career from high school to the presidency of a medium-sized corporation. That may be right for him, but I could use a little elasticity.

You must be ready for surprises. It is foolish to miss the obvious clues of disaster. It is wise to prevent accidents and to avoid poor performance. A rigid plan can hamper your ability to respond quickly to change. Blind chance does play a part. New opportunities appear, but you have to be able to see them. That may not happen if you are totally caught up in a particular plan for the future. The house on the hill, the presidency, the prize for being perfect. You will need to look hard at the goals that cannot be altered, the questions that you avoid. You may literally be killing yourself by investing so much of yourself in a future goal. When you are a prisoner of your own illusion of what life might be, you miss the opportunity to experience the present.

The paradox of setting goals is that you must plan with total commitment and yet be ready for the unexpected to disrupt your plans completely. If you believe that your answer lies in your plans, your profession, a person, a place, or an idea, then you are condemning yourself to endless disillusionment. Your answer is in those things and it is not.

This means that you need to be general in your approach to the future but very specific and direct about how you deal with the present. When you focus on what matters to you, you can ask "What can I do now, this week, this month that will strengthen the main themes of my life?" Your specific future plans may never become realized, but that is all right if what you achieve satisfies important impulses.

Career planning is a process. The content can be irrelevant, depressing, and even foolish. That is all right. The processes of planning, of exploring options, of making decisions, taking action and evaluating the results are what matter.

Factors beyond our control form the future. Ill health, technological change, accidents, economic collapse, social upheaval, war, and calamity can destroy your plans. This never absolves you, however, from the responsibility for developing your talents and directing your energies toward the achievement of worthwhile goals. A self-directed career-planning program can enable you to keep looking at your work. You can change goals. Everybody deserves a fresh break now and then. What you must do is maintain a tenuous balance between present and future.

Social science truisms will keep you in good stead:

People who understand their self-interest make better career decisions than those who do not.

People who have more knowledge about options and resources make better career decisions than those who do not.

If you find that money has become important to you and you are in a low-paying field, a serious change may be necessary. On the other hand, you may realize that you value the free time that your present job affords you to spend with your family. If so, you will feel a lot better about your job and be reluctant to seek more responsibility and authority.

All of your life, regular progress checks will allow you to make appropriate decisions in time to avoid danger. New enthusiasms, new and missing people can alter your priorities. No plan lasts forever. You need to explore, extend, and correct your plan regularly. Perhaps monthly, at your appointments with yourself on Friday afternoon, make a point of checking both your short- and long-range thinking. You can compare your progress with your expectations and take corrective action as appropriate. This way you will avoid unpleasant surprises and have a better time. "Getting there," as the Cunard Lines used to say, "is half the fun." You may discover that the harbor is not the main event, the journey is what is really important.

Seven

All the Help You Can Get

SELECTING AND DEVELOPING TALENT

If you are going to flip something, you must have the courage of your convictions.
JULIA CHILD

Hurry up, please. It's time.
T. S. ELIOT

You do need help. None of us can do it alone. It is up to you to be a talent scout looking for people with promise, the desire to do well, natural ability, and evidence of taking advantage of whatever opportunity has been available to them. To do your job, you must both select and develop people. Everyone agrees that these are important matters, but in most organizations little is done about them. They are further examples of jobs that belong to everybody but are completed by none. Your organization requires a number of people to accomplish the work. There is more to be done than you can do yourself. You need to be sure that the work of each person and unit meets certain standards, is related to each other, and to the total effect.

When you have a position to fill, your first question should be "Why?" What would be the worst thing that would happen if you didn't fill the job? If the position is chief payroll clerk, dishwasher, or trash collector, you should fill it without delay. Few other job vacancies will be so pressing.

We tend to think of jobs as real, concrete entities. They are not. A job is merely a series of activities that an individual performs at a particular time and place. What may further characterize a job as a job is that it takes up enough time to become part of the individual's identity. We speak, therefore, of a manager, a systems planner, a homemaker, a radiologist, a typist. What happens in organizations is that job boundaries appear to be taut wire fences enclosing a tight little territory. Those lines were drawn to achieve certain goals. Perhaps those objectives are valid but they need to be examined periodically. Otherwise we trap ourselves into continuing to design systems and procedures for problems that no longer exist. When you have a key position to fill—for secretary, supervisor, deputy director, vice-president—it is a good time to be certain that your system of jobs is solving your current problems. If it is not, rather than recruiting a new employee, you could renew your internal structure. This may be a time when you would have minimal disruption. Your observation of the work place as you tour and discover how people are working provides a basis for ensuring that your organization has the right division of labor to get the work done. If the structure is wrong, even sophisticated strategies will prove inadequate.

Studying your time logs and those of your key personnel can help you envision how things might be better. When you have a vacancy, you have an opportunity to redesign jobs and even to upgrade positions. Other managers might take on some higher-level tasks. This could free up other tasks to enhance clerical or professional positions. You might find that some tasks can simply be eliminated.

Many managers are afraid that if they eliminate a position they will never get it back. Building empires is their first priority. Experience confirms, however, that employees with too little to do create almost insoluble problems. Those employees worry that they will be caught. They fear that someone may discover that they have nothing to do. They become defensive, gold plate their jobs, and invade other people's territory. Gossip and complaints fill their day. They slow down the work and fail to enhance their manager's performance.

Lean management pays off. The manager who gives people real work to do, and who knows what they are doing, can control the work and put emphasis on methods to improve productivity.

If you have to cut staff or otherwise save money, you have an excellent opportunity. You can redistribute tasks among your available talent. Often, in hard times, you can upgrade your best people's jobs. You may also be able to give people preferred tasks and opportunities to learn new skills in lieu of money when there is no money to give.

Many managers shy away from job redesign because they are accustomed to the established categories. It is useful for you to realize that breaking out of traditional thinking about jobs requires little more than an understanding of what tasks need to be done, how much time they require, what other functions or distractions need to be considered, and what level of skill is necessary.

It may be that your job requires a private secretary to manage your appointments and meetings, to arrange conferences, to supervise personnel matters such as time keeping, vacation schedules, and sick leave. You may need to recruit for a project manager for construction, a new art gallery director, a vice-president for sales.

Once you have determined that you must select someone for the job, consider how you expect that person to contibute to your vision of the organization and your goals. Such a review is aimed at preventing stagnation and at helping you keep in touch with your needs and pressures. Turnover gives you opportunity for a fresh perspective. In most organizations, managers merely look for someone just like the person who left or someone totally different. Neither approach is necessarily best.

The recruiting process may require a task force, including personnel advisors, to list, telephone, and log candidate inquiries. They need to know the objectives of the job, your analysis of what the job needs, and the talents and capacities that would augur well for success. Charge those assisting you to look for a match between the vocational objective of the candidate and your position. They should know the skills and interests of value to you and your organization. Work with your personnel staff but don't abdicate responsibility to them. You need to enter the process early and stay with it all the way. If you fail to focus on what you need and want, a series of people—unqualified for your position—will pass through the screening process with no one sure of what is happening. You will, as a result, lose time and foster stagnation and drift.

In hiring and promoting people, you are looking to what is going to be and not what has been. This means that you have to overcome unconscious stereotyping, especially of women, older workers, minorities, members of ethnic groups, and the handicapped. No one ever said it would be easy. No tests tell us who or what has the future in its marrow.

Whenever possible, have a peer panel or panel of managers review resumes, interview, and make recommendations. Many organizations require such a process. The panel performs best if you can be clear about what the position requires and if you forcefully direct them to make as wide a search as possible. A diversified work force reflects our national strength. When a search is limited by sex, race, age, or any other factor, you limit the talent pool. When a major educational organization announced an opening for the director of their tutoring program, they said that they needed an energetic young person. An advisor convinced them that they needed a person with vitality who could identify with and promote a program to aid young people with reading problems. They hired a retired school superintendent whose energy amazes and delights them. He had proven success as an educator and fund raiser, knew everyone in education, empathized with the staff and students, and had the freshest ideas of all their candidates.

For some positions, you may be considering people who are reasonably well known to you. They may be members of the same professional organizations and have mutual friends. You may even have worked together in the past. This could lead you to unwise assumptions. You may believe that the person shares your world view, sense of mission, and commitment. Such assumptions could be dangerous. You need to ask specifically how he or she might plan and manage your program.

When you are interviewing for a significant executive position, you might ask candidates for their assessment of key issues that the organization will be facing in the next few years. It could be enlightening to find out what the candidate would like to be involved with and what factors he or she considers in planning work.

Although it goes against most managers' experience, a structured interview process can simplify your task, give you objective data to consider, and put the employment process into a more rational focus. You can devise questions that give you insights into the candidates' understanding of the organization's values, their management philosophy, their experience managing people, and in communication. You want to know about their ability to overcome obstacles, to meet challenges, to plan and to develop themselves and others. If you control the interview and note answers to these critical questions, you will be less taken in by someone who is persuasive but later proves to lack management aptitude (see Figure 30).

You could have a checklist of qualities that are important to you and your organization. In their answers and demeanor, you will want to look for examples of loyalty and commitment, a capacity for vigorous action, and a penchant for following through despite resistance. When candidates describe accomplishments, you will be able to detect even subtle signs of inherent power. You can search for a purposefulness that permeates the candidate's description of activities. How well does he or she make intentions clear, demonstrate determination and commitment to goals? As you interview, observe carriage, speech, and choice of answers as signs of self-confidence.

Despite our best intentions, unknown blind spots can distort our view. As we interview we may ignore what is happening, forget important questions, and inhibit our curiosity. We may just pay no attention to inconvenient and embarrassing facts. Every organization has people doing jobs for which they are ill-equipped. People with no gift for leadership, who can't and won't lead, are in managerial positions. Corporate closets are full of hiring mistakes that no one acknowledges or corrects. They could fix them if they wanted to.

Review your career and highlight your most significant assignments?

What made those particular assignments important to you?

What are the key issues that you see this organization facing in the next few years?

What experience and knowledge do you have that would enable you to deal effectively with one or more of these issues?

What do you find most challenging about managing people?

What is your present approach to and experience in representing the organization with external groups?

Should you be appointed to this position, what are the most critical factors that you would consider in your planning?

Figure 30.   Structured interview for an executive.

In one family-held business, a man was hired because of his long and close relationship with the family. They needed professional management which they thought their friend would bring. He had worked for twenty years for a large corporation famous for its management methods. Shortly after he was hired, they realized that because he lacked supervisory aptitude, he had been left in a narrow staff-specialty for years. Five years later, the division that he manages has experienced a severe decline in productivity, a rise in turnover, absenteeism, and a spectacular grievance case which the company lost. The president and his brother, who is executive vice-president, do nothing but complain privately.

They cannot face the idea that such sharp businessmen could have made such a mistake. Fatuous overconfidence led them to believe that they would always make wise choices. They could fix it if they wanted to. They don't.

Their experience confirms research by Leon Festinger and others that, once an activity is launched, people tend to retain thoughts that are in harmony with it and to discard less harmonious thoughts. To look at the evidence can be embarrassing, to ask crucial questions and to take action becomes almost impossible.

Many people make serious errors in hiring and selecting people. They fail because they neither ask hard questions nor pay absolute attention to what is being communicated. If you ask people what assignments or activities have given them the most satisfaction, you can learn a lot about what matters to them.

When four people cite building a tree house as significant childhood accomplishments, this does not imply that building the house is necessarily what mattered. Nor could you infer that the accomplishment meant the same to each. One man who built a tree house at twelve says that the meaning of the tree house was that he persuaded his father to let him build his structure on a high rather than a low safe branch. His adult life confirms the pleasure he has always found in selling—whether an idea or a product. He recognizes that managing salespeople would take him away from that direct and pleasurable challenge. Another's recollection of his tree house adventure revolves around its do-it-yourself quality. He earned and saved the money, designed and built the tree house entirely on his own. He remembers his pride in doing it himself. For a while he worked unhappily in a managerial role before returning with relief to his laboratory. The third tree house builder had read *Tom Sawyer* before undertaking the project. He organized the other children in the neighborhood to do the work while he supervised. The fourth did find her calling in building houses. Her design was so attractive that it was featured in a Sunday newspaper supplement. Today she manages a small architectural firm where her ability to design quickly gives her the time to work with clients as well as manage employees.

One accomplishment does not signify a career. You need to find a pattern, and that is seldom easy. You may, however, notice that someone being interviewed for a management position cites no examples of selecting and developing people, resolving equal opportunity issues, working out employment problems. You might be wary of selecting someone for a leadership role who seems to prefer working alone.

When someone being interviewed for a position as manager cannot specifically describe what is rewarding about managing people, warning signals should go off in your head. One personnel manager says, however, that he'll hire the first person who doesn't say, "I like to work with people." You don't have to like working with people, you need to have stamina and willingness to instruct, listen, clarify, nag, demand, pay attention, and involve people in what must be done. Liking is nice but the ability to work effectively with people is what matters.

Interviewing is a dangerous game. Some studies indicate that most of us make decisions in the first sixty seconds of the interview. We, then, often without knowing it, ask questions that support our initial impression. If we find someone that we like, our questions allow the person to shine. Similarly, if the first minute or so gives us a negative impression, we ask questions that consciously or unconsciously reinforce that opinion. A major medical school doing a study of their students, looked at the relationship between interview results and success in medical schools. They found a negative correlation, but that hasn't stopped them from interviewing. Despite its inefficiency, no one knows what else to do. When you do interview, your questions need to be augmented by your assessment of the candidate's self-confidence, use of humor, and ability to communicate frankly, openly, and quickly establish trust.

Some people design interviews to see how others deal with stress. A person sent to a room for an interview waited for ten minutes. She considered going back to check with the receptionist, when someone suddenly jumped out from under the desk. She had the presence of mind to say, "Oh, a stress interview, how interesting. I've always wondered what they were like. What's next?" She also had the sense not to pursue employment with that organization. Less manipulative methods will give you better information about how people deal with difficult situations. It is unnecessary to seat people where sunlight blinds them, in a chair that wobbles, or at a distance where speech is uncomfortable.

You are, after all, looking for a colleague, not an adversary. The relationship that you establish at the interview will carry over into your work relationship. For that reason, it is useful to begin a dialogue with anyone you seriously consider hiring. Executive recruitment consultants often advise clients to control the questions and give little information. They, however, do not have to live with the employee. A good interview should provide the necessary information on your candidate's experience and goals as they relate to you and your organization, but potential employees need information, too. If you structure your interview, you can allow time for your own questions as well as time to expound on your organization's philosophy and style. You could clarify your concept of what is important, of what your organization regards as the main event. You can observe closely and concentrate on the candidate's reaction and identification with your mission and goals.

After the interview, write down your assessment while impressions are sharp (see Figure 31). It is your responsibility to judge if the person is and will be someone you can use. Your organization is not what it was ten years ago or last year. Neither are the people whom you consider. Organizations and people change all the time.

After interviews, you also should call people who have worked *over*, *with*, and *for* the candidate. Prepare your questions. Make notes and ask the same questions of different people. Move quickly to make a decision once you have your information. Set a deadline and meet it or be early. No matter how hard you try, you need to realize that our minds have a curious capacity to be conscious and unconscious of something at the same time. Honorable and sincere people know that they promote policies that are partially deceitful. We procrastinate on difficult decisions. We push the inconvenient questions out of our minds. Nothing will guarantee that this person will be a winner. Nor will any test certify that hiring this person will be good for the organization. You can only assess whatever evidence you can gather. Again, if all else fails, listen to your stomach, but your attention and concentration should make it unlikely that you will blunder into disaster.

The answers to your interview questions should tell you a good deal about how your candidates define problems, dig for a range of solutions, and analyze different possibilities. Your refer-

---

What evidence do I have of this person's effectiveness—mature judgment, hard work, achievement?

What significant achievements indicate talent, contributions to excellence, productivity.

What proof is there that this person will undertake moderate risks?

Why does the person want the job?

Do the person's job objectives fit the organization's objectives?

What challenges the person about the job?

What evidence do I have that the person is growing into someone whom we can use?

Figure 31. Post-interview assessment.

---

ence checks and interviews enable you to examine how your candidates deal with others. For managerial jobs you need people who emerge as leaders or influential members of work groups. You are looking for those whose advice and counsel is sought, who seek opportunity to lead. If you find these attributes, you have discovered a manager.

Developing your people at work requires as thoughtful a process as selection. People generally start a new job with enthusiasm. How they feel a year later is largely up to you. Your work in clarifying your values and the values of the organization enables you to say what it means to be a member of the organization. When rules are clear, life is easier. Adherence to a few simple values enables you to emphasize ways to bring your organization's themes to life.

If you cover every inch of your organization regularly, you will know what people are doing, where every penny goes, who is griping about what. If you make employees do things over when their first attempt is inadequate, they should learn a lot. There are people who look as if they are doing a good job and there are those who do it. Their achievement is worth your care and effort.

Your example is the most important development tool that your employees have. Be an example. Your emphasis on excellence, your efforts to stay abreast of technological change, to improve your managerial skills, and to learn from new ideas and people mean more than lectures on development. If you demonstrate your loyalty and dedication to the organization's values, you will encourage similar commitment from others. Your example of taking appropriate risks and making decisions helps your subordinates know what matters. If you show them that objectivity and openness are valued, they will make similar efforts. Your focus on the main event enables them to put energy where it counts.

Looking at people in terms of what it means to be a member of your organization—promoting certain values and important themes—enables you to see areas for development. If product leadership and excellence are your organization's themes, how does this show in the organization—in total—and in the smaller units—the individual jobs? What do your subordinates do that integrates such a policy into practice? Do plans and activities emphasize promotion of product excellence? What do your practices communicate?

Your own career development planning and continuous analyses of progress may be all that some employers need for them to learn how to set and achieve appropriate goals. Others may need guidance in writing and administering performance plans. You may want to coach some people, provide others with new experiences or training. Everyone needs feedback on their accomplishments.

You could ask key people for their perceptions of their jobs and how they know when they are doing well. You could ask them to look at the skills that your organization requires. Developing the abilities of your subordinates is complex. Your ability as a coach is somewhat dependent on your natural inclination to help others succeed and on your own self-knowledge. It requires understanding of their strengths and yours as well as use of your experience and knowledge. Despite individual styles, successful coaching shares an emphasis on goal setting, scheduling, feedback, and support. Specifically, you might help employees learn to foster goal-commitment in their subordinates. You could coach them to make decisions, take risks, communicate effectively. Although you cannot create talent, you can teach people techniques that will allow them to use their talents more effectively (see Figure 32).

One manager increased productivity and developed his staff best by giving away his favorite tasks. He finds that he trains people best on jobs in which he feels invested. Also, this act forces him to look for new areas for his own growth and prevents complacency.

Another manager found when she studied her log that she could increase productivity by sticking to what she does best. She delegates other tasks and consciously rewards people for effectively handling the jobs she avoids. Basically, you need to discourage inflexibility, passivity, and traditional responses. If you don't, you risk creating a work environment that frightens away the very people you need.

If you are working with novice decision makers, try to remember how difficult it could be for them. They may be apprehensive and feel very lonely. Few decisions in organizations are made alone. No single person's information sources are adequate. Subordinates are often, understandably, impatient about their manager's indecision. They complain over coffee that no one takes action, that no one does anything. They see managers as full of power. As a manager, however, you see yourself burdened with responsibility. Often, as you know, any action that you take will cause pain. Your position may isolate you from information. You must depend on rumor, conversations, hunches. Such dependence goes against the grain.

Wise managers seek assistance from many sources. They search for the root causes of problems rather than merely deal with the symptoms. If you consult with your subordinates in this process, they will learn that decisions are not made in a vacuum. That alone can be a vital part of their development.

Encourage people to:
    Define objectives and goals precisely.
    Put emphasis on important daily actions that lead to achievement.
    Take moderate risks.
    Remember that actions have consequences.
    Value their credibility.
Demand excellence of them.
Reward even small steps forward.
Review errors with the objective of being certain that the mistake is never made again.
Remind them to help other people.
Help them to aim for a bigger picture.

Figure 32.   Coaching.

A short time ago a young engineer was promoted to supervisor after less than a year in a large manufacturing plant. Everyone was pleased with her aptitude, her enthusiasm, her progress, and hard work. She was the first and only woman in the plant in a supervisory job. Within a short time she felt apprehensive. If she asked for help, would they think she shouldn't be supervisor? If she didn't ask for help, would she have good information? Her anxiety grew. She was alone. No one helped her assess the possible outcomes of decisions, examine the benefits and risks of certain actions, and establish what the worst possible outcome would be if she were to fail. Her manager thought that she needed no help. He had never had a woman supervisor before and felt unsure of what to do. Productivity and morale in her section were high, so he left her alone. Other people thought that she was doing fine. They told one another, but no one told her. Unknown to them, her discomfort grew. She felt more and more disoriented, uncertain of how much risk to take. She was unsure of what was important and what she could get fired for. When she abruptly resigned, they were shocked. At last report, she had gone sailing. Racing in international competition provides her with direct information, coaching, and feedback that teach her to make decisions and to take risks.

Many managers don't talk to their employees about their careers because they fear that they will raise false expectations. It is not my experience that career advising raises expectations. Not too many people harbor hopes for an unrealizable future. A few do. No one has to raise their expectations, their unreality is their unreality. If you ignore the desert, it doesn't go away. Some people with no aptitude for working with people aspire to management titles. They are basically interested in the position and the perquisites—not the work. Many people just believe that they are doing better than they are.

Career planning does not invent ambition but does, in my experience, enable people to be more realistic about the future. The focus is on people taking responsibility for their own growth. I find that most people respond positively to efforts that assist them with their self-understanding. Most want to expand their knowledge of their preferences and their resources. They respond positively to the idea that there are methods and people to help them focus on what is really important.

Initially, I was surprised when most people in career planning programs developed more interest in their own jobs than in seeking a new career. The majority work to strengthen their skills on the job. They find ways to better use their abilities and shore up weaknesses. Growth is not always upward. Career development can result in efforts toward lateral growth: adding new skills, learning more about the business, becoming more adept in areas of strength. Some people develop new interests and explore. Others build on old and neglected skills. A few, even, decide that the organization is the wrong place for them. When they leave, they benefit as well as the organization. The thrust of career development is on: "What do you want to do?" not "What do you want your title to be?"

Certain common attributes and values link effective executives. Although there are no cookbooks for leadership, or easy answers for executives, evidence is accumulating that leaders do understand and are committed to translating policy into action, and that they value technical competence and depth. They speak effectively for the organization and direct projects within appropriate constraints of time, money, and effort. You can measure your employees in terms of their ability to achieve similar standards.

It is easier to go from *good* to *better* or *best* than to go from *poor* to *good*. Emphasizing your employee's strengths pays off in expenditure of effort and in results. If you have a manager with a gift for communication and diplomacy, her performance plan should give her more scope in these areas. You could schedule her to present briefings, to represent the organization at conferences. She could be encouraged to take a larger role in union or government relations.

A manager who shows ability in developing organizations might be assigned to strengthen a weak but vital department and its discouraged staff. The manager with a talent for finance and resource management could investigate the possible acquisition of a consumer goods manufacturer. These assignments serve the organization and develop management skills.

You probably see negative behavior that you would like to eliminate. One manager fails to inform you of his activities. You are unpleasantly surprised in senior staff meetings from time to time when you hear of incidents that you should have known about. Another fails to delegate. She continues to write the presentations that her writers should prepare, she enjoys going off with the photographers to select sites for advertising campaigns. She arranges interviews that her secretary should handle.

A third continues as salesman and keeps all the best accounts. When his sales people go out on a sales call, he always finds time to go along to give them confidence and to answer questions that they can't handle. He introduces his sales personnel in glowing terms. He says that they are his stars. Their ability to shine is unproved since at meetings with customers, they are scarcely allowed to speak. He fields the questions, turns on his charm, and behaves as if the customers belonged to him. The men and women who work for him merely write up the orders.

The first thing to ask is, does it matter? Your production division is producing. The public relations office is promoting, the sales department is selling. What is wrong is the managers are not managing. If you look closely you will see that the production manager doesn't report on action because he doesn't really understand a new technical function which is under his direction. A long-needed internal communication program has never been initiated by the public relations department. Employees in all three departments feel stifled and frustrated. Their effectiveness reduced, some have tried to communicate that they want more responsibility. Even blunt messages don't get through. Most of the employees are circulating resumes. Others play computer games when no one is watching.

If the situation is to change, you have to act. Your managers will have to see that there is a pay-off to development, to delegation, to eliminating clutter, to letting employees in on the action. You will need to show them that developing people is an essential part of their jobs.

A conscious effort at career development can serve many purposes. One is that the process can help you identify future leaders. Career development provides a test of their intelligence, energy, ability to analyze and synthesize, judgment, decision-making skills, and ability to win other people's respect. Trust, respect, and risk provide the background for growth and development.

At the Jewel Corporation, young talents are assigned to a vice-presidential sponsor. What may be unique about the Jewel approach is that the managers are not bosses, but the "first assistants" of those who report to them. The organization chart is turned upside down. The manager leads by coaching, listening, and teaching. They are rewarded by helping others to get things done. It is not their job to do and change the organization. That is pretty risky. At Jewel they bet on the talent of their younger people. The mentors risk emotional involvement in working closely with their juniors. Such risk may not pay off. Abraham Zaleznik points out in his work on leadership that the willingness to take risks appears to be crucial in developing leaders.

Who can you stretch? A secretary, offered a position as clerical trainer, was initially frightened at the opportunity. She decided, however, that if her manager believed that she could do it, she could do it. Today she manages the operation. A bored management analyst was asked if he'd like to try marketing. Others saw his potential. He trusted their belief in his abilities. His knowledge of the business, memory, and ability to gain people's respect contributed to a long string of corporate sales records.

Your job is to encourage risk and growth. First, show the way yourself, then provide support. Applaud jerky steps forward and arrange for small successes to keep people going. If someone fails, applaud the attempt. Analyze quickly and correct the situation. You should talk with your subordinates about what new responsibilities they would like to assume and why. You will discover that not everyone wants to be company president. In one organization when they closed the major division, they asked the senior managers what problems they would like to work. Everyone drew up a solid working plan that today is making or saving considerably more money than it cost.

Avoid the example of organizations that throw away project managers as if they came by the carton. No one gives thought to what they will do next. They themselves give no time to considering the futurity of their present decisions. A manager who demonstrates talent for productivity and managing people can be used in other divisions. Often no one knows or thinks of that manager because he or she never did a particular job. It is as if we would not hire people to fly to Mars because they had never done that sort of work before.

In an organization where career planning was part of the weekly staff meetings, a supervisor, wanting a bigger role, began to work on her fear of addressing large groups. She took on more speaking assignments, gained confidence, and began long-range plans to prepare for a managerial position. Another person in the organization found that no one had recognized his aptitude for improving procedures. He sought opportunities to demonstrate these skills and let others know about his ability. He found that he needed to communicate what was important to him if he was to be taken seriously. Another, a program manager nearing retirement, was so encouraged by others on the staff that within a year she successfully doubled the number of seminars that she was running. She also planned a research project for her retirement. When the time came, she made the project a reality.

It may be that such planning enables people to prepare for change in society, in organizations, and in themselves. This may allow us to cope with the accelerating change that quickly makes some jobs obsolete and creates others yet unknown. The activity also strengthens the psychological contract between individuals and the organization. It facilitates a more open climate and is an aid to developing work and special project teams.

Career planning activities may indicate to employees that management is involved in efforts to overcome the impersonal nature of modern organizations. People experience a demonstration of the larger social responsibility of a mature organization. A criterion of such an organization may be that it is attuned to the larger community, and thus recognizes that organizations are developed by people to serve people.

The psychological contract is summed up in plans that describe what the employees will do and how you will know that they are doing well. Performance planning can be done yearly or every six months and need not be a lengthy or painful process.

With some practice, you can write a performance plan in thirty minutes (see Figure 33). The first step is your own plan. Then you

---

Take notes on:

Where individual's responsibilities support my performance plan.

How I know when the employee is doing well.

Employee's strengths which are important to the organization's mission and goals.

Activities and training that would enhance strengths.

What could make a difference: job modification, new assignment, training, feedback.

How effectively employee:
Keeps me informed.
Provides me with completed staff work.
Recommends solutions to problems.
Stays up-to-date.
Develops subordinates.
Meets deadlines.
Produces high quality work in quantity.
Works with others.

Figure 33. Performance plan checklist.

---

look at the roles of your employees. Their job is to make you look good, to support your major projects. Their plans should center on what you would recognize as the mark of an effective employee. For example, a project manager's performance hinges on her being able to instantly give accurate information about her major projects, subprojects, budget, and goals. Similarly, her subordinates must be able to provide her with necessary information on procurement, costs, staffing, procedures, task progress, and proposed solutions to problems. Everyone has responsibilities that matter and can be measured. People who work for you need to review the status of their work. They should report and recommend action, provide you with necessary oral, written, or computer reports, and proposals for improvement. It is their job to oversee, update, and maintain programs, systems, and procedures. If they have subordinates, their job includes recommendation of work experience, development, and training assignments.

Perhaps your division is slated to show a marked increase in sales, or you are to develop a new national program to reach mothers of young children, or to implement a system to aid the corporation in planning for the succession of executives. You, then, look to see who will help you in this endeavor and how you can measure their efforts. You ought to be able to identify other tasks that maintain and enhance your organization's major themes. Cost reduction and winning are signs of productivity improvement. You want to consider new projects for people to undertake, maintenance that needs improvement, clutter that should be eliminated. Reflect on the questions these ideas imply and figure out what you want people to do and how you would measure their progress.

Before discussing this with employees, have them write up their proposed performance plan. This will enable you to look at how you each perceive the job. Your employee may have valuable insights that could improve the plan. Some may have ideas beyond their ability or unrelated to the organization's goals and needs. Whatever information you gather is useful. The exercise helps you to ascertain if your employee understands the basis on which work will be judged. Dates and goals give you both something to measure.

You have the opportunity to reiterate that goals are not cast in concrete. New priorities mean that plans have to be rewritten. When dates slip, you want to be forewarned and involved in discussion of new deadlines. Performance plans can put emphasis on positive ways to achieve goals. Consequences of both action and inaction are made clear and a contract is established under which you and your employees can work.

You could determine that all would be right with the world when your production manager effectively supervises his new technical function and keeps you informed of what is happening in his division. To give him the hands-on experience that he needs, you may want to send him to work with the manufacturer of the new equipment for a focused orientation into the uses of the new technology. The public relations manager's plan can require her to prepare plans, projects, and schedules to improve promotion activities including implementation of that long-delayed internal communication program.

Your managers should be required to document and report procedures, accomplishments, and activities. This enables you to measure the time that your people spend in management activity. Sometimes only threats of demotion to salesmen, writers, or production workers will make supervisors take management responsibilities seriously. When it comes to motivation, some executives find no substitute for fear.

Most people, however, are primarily motivated by achievement. As a manager who always tries to do a good job, you can empathize with the needs of those who work for you. Studs Terkel in *Working* describes a waitress who knows that she is doing well when she puts down a plate and it doesn't make a sound.

Achievement and recognition motivate people—what some call "Bright Lights and Trumpets." Some first-line supervisors act as if they have no knowledge of such obvious principles. They underrate how much people desire to help the organization achieve its goals. If they learn supervision by trial and error, you may end up with too much error. Their performance plans should provide ways for them to learn the skills they need to properly direct and stimulate their employees. Although supervisory or management training for them may be a warning rather than a reward, it may be necessary if you are to save the sanity of their subordinates. All too often, employees feel helpless and controlled by the events and the people around them. The organization, the rules, the way work is organized, can make people feel manipulated and misunderstood.

Sometimes people feel that they are not growing, and they see no possible change. People who work for you may feel stuck. As a result they may have problems maintaining enthusiasm and making a maximum contribution to the organization. This often happens to people when they have been in a job too long. Some are stuck at a fairly high level, apparently as a function of age. It is wasteful if their skills are unused. People who are no longer considered for special assignments or are left out of policy-making decisions may retire on the job. You may suspect that they are dreaming of escape and notice that they complain a lot. You could look around for problems that they might solve. You could ask them what project might interest them. This is where having a strong grasp of the organization's mission is useful. Ask yourself:

What would they do differently?

How can I connect what they would like to do with the organization's mission and requirements?

Your goal is to brighten your world as well as theirs.

People avoid being a nothing, manipulated, unappreciated, and controlled. We all want to be somebody, self-determined, appreciated, and self-controlled. It's not your job to direct someone else's career. With the best intentions, you may steer them in the wrong direction. You want them to be active and to assume responsibility. Healthy and stable self-esteem rests on work that the individual finds worthwhile. Interference with this wisdom can result in frustration, irritability, fatigue, and a feeling of entrapment. Sometimes you need to step back to see what you are doing and how your actions toward subordinates are being perceived. No matter how well you think you are doing, others may think otherwise.

When we're at work, the focus is on getting the work done. It is hard to find time to think about experiences that will enable people to develop. However, if you don't you won't have successors when you move on. You won't have people with the skills that the new technologies demand. Your organization won't be ready for change. No matter how hard it is, you need to look at what people are doing, how their performance is enabling you to achieve your goals and mission, and what new experiences would allow them to develop. Although most managers know that development of subordinates is useful and important, the majority find it a burden. It is hard to say much against developing people, but doing something is another matter.

Although it would be a mistake to slavishly copy Japanese methods, we are always interested in pragmatic solutions. Perhaps we can learn from Japanese organizations in which management styles emphasize human relations and where managers are rewarded primarily for developing subordinates and for giving their supervisors emotional support.

Although training is what many think career development is all about, training ought to be your last resort. The most effective course is to develop people through the work itself. This needs to be augmented by planning, regular and useful feedback, and timely evaluation which is tied to development of strengths and eradication of shabbiness.

Finding the time is the hardest part of the process. Many managers want to develop their subordinates but never get around to it. They may even know that their own promotion depends on developing a replacement. Yet, in no time, the week is over, the quarter has ended, and the new year is upon them. This hard fact provides yet another argument for eliminating clutter and finding ways to concentrate on real concerns. Survival really matters. Survival depends on people trained, able, and willing to carry on the enterprise.

Time becomes a problem with performance appraisal. Rigidity is usually the rule. Once a year in June or September, the manager and employee sit opposite one another for an awkward session. Rarely does management integrate the development of the work force into the organic ebb and flow of the organization. In a production organization, September may start with a high scream. The work situation becomes more shrill until January, when there is a mild lull before spring. Another push then begins which lasts until July. In another organization, the board of director's meetings on the second Thursday of the month determine the rhythm. During the first two weeks of the month, people compile charts, prepare reports, and practice presentations. During the beginning of the third week they rest briefly before the next round. In a government office, the cycle builds to the August budget review and preparation of congressional testimony. Other organizations may just go with no pauses until the play opens, the product is introduced, or the rocket is launched.

A performance review should contain no surprises. It is a major error to review only once a year. A performance review should be the final act of a continuous review process and the first act of the next performance plan.

You may have lulls in the morning before the mail arrives or in the late afternoon when the market has closed or the paperwork is finished. You can find time to let people know how they are doing. Most people remain too busy because they are uncomfortable about telling subordinates what impressions they create on others. Such exchanges make many people nervous, so they avoid the whole thing. You can be scrupulous about not hurting people's feelings or pride, but all along you may be crippling them.

In mature relationships, people use openness and candor to prevent communication barriers from getting in the way. Openness and candor, however, are not the goals. The goal is to be useful (see Figure 34). It is risky. Timing, what you say, and how you say it are factors to consider. Unless you learn how to give feedback and unless you do it regularly and often, you won't be able to monitor the work of your organization. There is simply no other way. Evaluation can't be kept secret if it is to do any good.

You might find it useful to review what you want to say and how you will say it. Feedback is intended to be helpful to the recipient. This means that the other person must understand what you are saying, be willing to accept your view and able to do something about it. You may have to be wary of venting hostility. The line between constructive and destructive criticism is almost invisible. Blaming someone for a mistake is less effective than making sure it never happens again.

Feedback must be specific. With the talkative employee you can say, "When you ramble on, I lose sight of what you are trying to tell me." You have given the employee a specific area to look at. He may choose to go on rambling, but he will make a choice.

Feedback ought to be timely. You can remember something that happened two minutes ago more vividly than something that happened a week ago. If right after the meeting you say,

"You were doing fine until you mentioned repaving the parking lot. I saw her eyes glaze over then." The other person may be able to remember and to explore more effective behavior.

Sometimes it can be very difficult to accept criticism. There are times when people don't want to face what is being said to them. If you don't believe that the organization or the people care about you, or if you distrust their motives, you will seldom accept anything they say. How people talk to you also makes a difference. If the other person's tone, expression, and choice of words express hostility, you are not likely to accept what they say. If someone rattles off criticism without even looking at you, you are likely to feel judged and ill-treated, no matter what the intention was.

You can simply learn to describe what you have seen and the effect it had on you. One manager told me he has learned a phrase that is now automatic. He says: "This may be my problem and not yours; however, I want you to know that I am uncom-

---

The objective is utility, not openness and candor.

DESCRIPTIVE
I saw . . .
I heard . . .
I reacted . . .

TIMELY
Refers to a specific incident.
Given as soon as possible after the incident.

USEFUL
Information is something the person is willing,
ready, and able to do something about.
It is not overwhelming. No more than 2 or 3 comments.

Figure 34.   Feedback.

---

fortable when you act. . . ." He goes on to describe the situation with specific references to time and place. After months of practice he has learned to close his mouth after completing his description. He wages a continuing fight against the temptation to extrapolate on how foolish, obstinate, and immature the other person is. He is finally being rewarded by employees who listen, accept, and have even changed their behavior as he changes his.

Sometimes timing is impossible. People who behave badly on the job may be distraught, confused, and so upset that they aren't ready to receive feedback when the incident occurs. The danger is that with passing time, you may have to write it off. If you complain six months later, you will sound vindictive. If, however, the same employee keeps repeating similar actions in a similar defensive state, you have another problem.

Feedback that people ask for is more likely to be received in an open state of mind than feedback that is not requested. You must be prepared to give specific information to those who ask you, "How did you feel about the way I worked with the technical people on that problem? Did you see me working in an appropriate way or would you have liked me to involve you more in the process?" Such a question requires more than "You did a good job." You have an opportunity to frame future work behavior and open communication with your subordinate.

Such a solicitation is probably genuine and you lose nothing if you treat it openly and with confidence. Look back at the situation, recall it vividly. Perhaps you felt slighted and left out or maybe, instead, you felt pride in your employee's good judgment. Either way, such information can be useful to both of you.

No one gets too much approval. Be wary of those who ask for negative feedback, who say that they want to know everything that you don't like about them. They are probably lying. I have watched it happen again and again. If you tell them what you see as the truth, they will never forgive you.

I had someone advise me once to say five good things every day to those who worked with me. He rightly surmised that I simply believed that they were aware of my high regard for them. I was not used to praise and had little practice giving it. It is still not easy, but it is worth the effort. When you tell people what you see them doing well, you encourage their best behavior. The secretary whose telephone manners are exemplary will only get better if you let her know that you appreciate how well she screens and places your calls. If she does a good job at routing calls to others who can answer for you, she is cutting clutter. When she demonstrates that courtesy is never out of date, her behavior enhances you and the organization. You can also tell your boss what he or she does well. If you make a point of looking for specific positive feedback to five people a day, you will be identifying skills that will help you do your work, encourage growth, and improve the organization's health.

If you tell someone that you don't like his attitude, what are you saying? If someone said that to you, you wouldn't know what they were referring to or where to start. If you say to someone, "I get irritated when you finish my sentences for me," the issue is clear. Telling someone she should be more persuasive is not helpful. You should figure out specifically what she does that makes you feel that way. You may decide that she needs to organize her thoughts better before she makes a presentation. That's useful because she can do something about it. She can learn to identify her objective and determine what points support that idea. If she practices, she may be able to present her arguments more forcefully. Someone who says "Okay?" fifty times in a three minute presentation will seldom believe your feedback, but later if he hears himself using this verbal crutch he may do something about it.

You may decide not to say anything. The timing is seldom right and it is risky. Many managers fear making mistakes, so they say nothing. Being cautious is risky, too. The test is to ask if your feedback will be specific, timely, descriptive, and useful. Sometimes those are hard criteria to meet. The alternative may be to say nothing. I would argue for prudent risk. Be more open than closed. Experiment to see what happens. If you mean to be helpful but clumsiness wins, in all probability no one will die. You can say that you feel clumsy—and you will instantly feel more assured. You don't have to be perfect.

The other person may, like Popeye, respond, "I yam what I yam." He or she is right. We have the right to be who we are and no one has the right to dictate to us what we should be like.

When you give feedback, you must remember that other people have the right to evaluate what they hear, decide what to believe and do with the information. Acceptance or rejection is up to them. Your purpose in giving feedback is to enable them to receive the most useful information you can give. This allows people to judge how they are doing and how they might be more effective.

Your primary goal in developing people is to create an environment in which those who work with you can identify their preferences and work to improve their skills. The healthy atmosphere is one in which their self-confidence allows them to act on their experience and intuition even when that action differs from what others around them believe is right. Your effort with employees should reinforce your attention to the main event, your emphasis on meeting deadlines, doing completed staff work, and their role in making you look good. When people want to be promoted, you can help them to know the obvious—that they need to be first-rate at work.

It is realistic for you to ask "What's in it for me?" When you help competent, hard-working people to grow, you get better support and more time to concentrate on your job. Your productivity will rise, and you will be seen as someone who develops people. This can mean that you are more promotable yourself.

If you recognize the potential of your managers and groom them to move in the organization, you will become a tangible asset to your organization. When people fail to use talented employees, they waste natural resources. If you gain a reputation for developing people, talented people will want to work for you. You can also look upon such achievement with satisfaction. It pays to help as many people as you can. Someone whom you develop may even hire you one day. After all, we can use all the help we can get.

Eight

Know How to Do It

The game of Chinese baseball is almost identical to American baseball. . . . There is one and only one difference and that is: after the ball leaves the pitcher's hand and as long as the ball is in the air, anyone can move any of the bases anywhere.

R. G. H. SUI

Being solemn is easy. Being serious is hard.

RUSSELL BAKER

People who respect themselves are willing to accept the risk that the Indians will be hostile.

JOAN DIDION

The dailiness of your work erodes attention to the main event. Just when you think you are learning to keep your eye on the ball, you discover that your focus has interfered with your peripheral vision. If the bases have been moved, you can't be sure what the game is all about. In some of the more subtle forms of Chinese baseball, another base may have been added or hidden. An unrecognizable substitution may have been made.

In managing the main event, logic provides no help, rules fail, and prescriptions prove to be placebos. A professor of modern dramatic literature used to lean across the podium daily to say, "The key word is paradox." He might just as well have been talking about management and leadership.

No matter how valid your premises and deductions, you can only expect contradictions. Facts, hard work, and money help. Small disciplines help too, as do shared values, self-respect, attention, concentration, and concern for results. Nothing, however, is enough. The world is large, its problems are large, and our grasp of life is fragile. Paradox is the key. You have to keep your eye on the ball and the bases at the same time. You always need more facts, but "to get it right," as Ruth Gordon said, "you must never under any circumstances face the facts." If you do, you will be overwhelmed. You could find yourself being careless when you need to be careful and careful when you need to be carefree. It was Robert Frost who said: "Families break up when people take hints you don't intend and miss hints you do intend." So it is with organizations.

The hints are there beneath the surface. We need to pay attention to these hidden agendas, for they tell us something about other people's worlds. We must try to understand their perceptions because so many people seem determined to keep us from moving ahead and even, determined to take away whatever it is that we have. They break our sand castles for no reason. Whether careless or deliberate, these actions hurt. In Chinese baseball, if a base is moved by an act of sabotage or by someone who is indifferent to your game, the effect is the same. When some things are done, they can never be undone.

Although the news discourages you, you must keep it to yourself. Should you demonstrate a lack of faith in the organization, the program, or the people, you communicate the message that there is no point in trying. Your action counts. Your inaction counts too. What you could do is important. You can establish new behavior, learn new tricks, strive for elegance, even become a substantially different person. You can put your energy into achievement, into excellence, into the main event.

Elegant achievement, excellence, sounds like a lost cause. Maybe it is. But maybe it would be worthwhile to recover the ability to see that the emperor is wearing no clothes. Maybe lost causes are worth fighting for.

Look at the four-minute mile, the Copernican theory, the electric light, Hellenic thought, flight to the moon, the worth of the individual. After all, is struggling for a paycheck what it is about? It does matter to work for something that matters.

In searching for excellence, despite your best intentions, the clutter keeps getting out of control. The criticism given so carefully comes off contemptuously. Enterprises, as Joan Didion points out, do go bankrupt.

You have no choice. You are thrown back on yourself to play the game as best you can. Moaning does no good. Somehow it is up to you to keep things moving in the right direction, to get all the oars clicking at the same time. The clues are there, but we develop functional blindness. The results, as Henry Mintzberg and other management scientists describe, are executives whose days are devoid of planning. Their experience is characterized by problems thrust on them by superior and subordinate, by demands transmitted by telephone, crises generated through unexpected meetings and by unforeseen calamity.

Managers mistakenly believe that their job is to solve problems. Bill Oncken and Donald L. Wass in a classic article, "Management Time: Who's Got the Monkey?" describe a manager whose blindness is lifted one weekend as he realizes that he has assumed total responsibility for solving his organization's problems. While he is working in the office on Saturday morning, he sees his four key subordinates teeing up on the golf course. His subordinates have placed the "monkeys" on his back. All the next moves are up to him. This is no unique situation. Most managers generally end the week with a long list of unfinished tasks. Their employees, on the other hand, know a dozen ways to look busy when they have nothing to do. Some don't even bother to hide their inactivity.

Most employees and many managers have too little scope. They have been delegated neither responsibility nor authority. Those who lead the organization assume that it is their job to solve problems. What happens then has nothing to do with intelligent practice, adult behavior, or winning. People, given little opportunity to lead, are expected to follow instructions and to keep the flow moving. When managers are expected to follow rather than lead, they remain in an adolescent state. They act as if questioning the status quo will bring disaster. Many come to believe that there is nothing to question anyhow.

People want to be in charge but are ambivalent about authority. It is more fun to be the boss than to be a subordinate, but authority arouses surprising knee-jerk behavior. We are sometimes childish in our relations with the organizations for which we work. Few of us are ever wholly independent. Most of us are trapped by our need of money into dependence on an employer. Managers often encourage dependency. They like to feel that they are in control. Our own lust for independence pushes us to be free of that dependency. Reporters on big city papers dream of publishing a small weekly paper in the Carolinas. Government workers in the Department of Defense long to open a small business in Oregon. Manhattan advertising executives yearn to be lobstermen in Maine. The conflict between dependency and independence can keep us running in place. Some people passively submit. A few actively try to change the place in which they are. The difficulty is that organizations are pervasive, so good at socializing us, that individuals seldom bring about real change. There are, of course, humane generals and socially conscious bankers, but it is not easy. This desire to control causes many managers to overmanage, to control their employees. Indeed, many people think that controlling people is what management is about.

Leaders should have no time to control people. You're busy enough thinking, planning, discussing, interacting, suggesting, bargaining, negotiating, and checking. Controlling others is not the main event. It is less important than establishing objectives on which those who depend on you for a salary can focus. Your peripheral vision must allow you to see what is going on all around you.

If someone doesn't want to do what you want them to do, somehow they will manage to go their own way. Work is slowed, people quit, other projects become more important. I can't make others think the way I want them to or follow directions exactly as I intended. I can't make you understand my objectives, but if I keep defining and redefining organizational objectives, you may begin to understand what I am trying to do. If you begin to see that what we do matters, you may decide that it's worth the effort. If I believe that I am in control because you have accepted my ideas, then I am deluding myself. There is a lot of self-delusion in management. You can control people only when you intimidate them and remain there to keep up the pressure.

You are not paid to control people. Your job is not to make people jump. People do need to accept the terms of their employment but we are all entitled to a discussion of how to do the job, participate, disagree, and express ideas. Unless asked to do something dangerous or immoral, we should, of course, do as asked. The rule is to act first and file a grievance later.

Sometimes as manager, you lead. Sometimes others do. Leadership is functional in task-oriented situations. When the report is in its final stage, the typist may be the leader. The supervisor is not in control but is responsible and brings good judgment to the situation. It is best not to rely only on your own advice. Listen to others. The independence of those who work for you is key to your ability to deal with future problems. We need others to disagree, to give us other viewpoints. If they are free to disagree with you, you can believe them when they do agree.

One reason people want to control others is because they fear having others control them. They try to get there first. It is risky. You may work in a place where people keep trying to control you. This uses up time and energy unnecessarily. The manager who gives up control finds little need to control. There is less clock-watching, fewer sabotage attempts, less time given to unproductive behavior. By delegating both the symbols and realities of power to subordinates, the manager has more time for the real work of leadership: establishing and setting goals, evaluating progress.

If you just can't share authority, you may have to move on. Very often those who start an enterprise are the worst sort of managers when the organization begins to grow and stabilize. The behavior that leads to success when a business is starting out is often the behavior that causes failure later on. Success can force the entrepreneurial manager to depend on the professional manager to maintain the organization. When the organization needs a structure to keep production on target, you may need to bring in accountants to handle finance or an industrial engineer to handle production. New people could bring in a different approach to budgeting or a new way to look at potential markets. When organizations just grow, they often communicate by shouting, no other system is needed. As the organization becomes more complicated, you need more careful orchestration.

Many managers resist such change. They endlessly tell new people how it used to be. In the meantime, decisions go up for advice, back down for tinkering, then back up for approval. They may go to everyone else for concurrence. It takes forever. Decision making needs to be at the work level. When routine decisions go to top management, you have problems. As a good executive, you want your subordinates to make the routine decisions. When you delegate work, your responsibility isn't lessened. Good control systems rest in your hands. Prevention of shabbiness is your job.

You don't have to move on. You can turn yourself into an effective manager for the organization that yours is becoming. That's growth, but it takes pain, practice, and persistence.

Your job is to expect excellence, and those who work for you should expect excellence from you. Equality is a useful condition of excellence. Constraints hindering people must be removed if you would have them successfully solve problems in order to free you for managing the main event. When people are treated as beings of intrinsic worth, it provides a background on which your vision of the organization can be imposed. People benefit when they know what their purpose is. When they don't know that purpose, people often don't know what to do. Retreat is one response. Some people hide in hobbies. Others cling to unpleasantness. They accept what is happening as some sort of expected punishment. The leader's role is to spell out clearly understood purposes, to clarify a vision of a work place where good and worthwhile work is done. The purpose, as one manager put it, "may be to make a buck, but we should have a good time and feel good along the way." Injustice and imperfection are deviations and not expressions of corruption. As a manager, you want to keep that vision in mind and find ways to help others see what you see. Your words can create pictures and evoke ideas that sound familiar and right. Words, diagrams, and models enable you to make your vision more concrete so that others can share it. Your resolve generates nerve—your nerve and other people's nerve.

People will be watching you, however, and will be asking themselves if what you say is what you mean. If there is uncertainty, the decision will go against you. They will believe that you mean something else and will wonder what that might be. That is why effective executives are the ones who say what they mean and mean what they say. Their action confirms their words.

It could be that your most crucial decision is to let others decide. Surrendering control can be difficult. Other people won't run things the same way that you have, but delegation is key to increased productivity. It is your lever (see Figure 35).

Many managers never delegate. Convinced that no one else can do the job, they'd rather do it themselves. Some feel that no one else is equally motivated, conscientious, or hardworking. They believe that others have no good ideas anyway. Even should that be true, unless you delegate, unless you teach people to be conscientious and hardworking, unless you nurture their ideas, they won't be able to help you. If you are to increase productivity, you need help. If you think that you are the only person with good ideas, you are practicing self-deception. You are holding to archaic canons of authoritarian management that can only impede your progress.

Delegation is necessary and risky. People will do things differently. Your instructions will probably be misunderstood. What you say is likely to be different from what they hear. They may not see the diagram that you draw the same way as you perceive it. Their grasp of the subject will be different and may not express your own. You need to know, when you give instructions, what the other person plans to do. It is important that you find out what people are doing. You can merely stop by them at work to ask, "How's it coming?" This makes it clear that you care, that this is a main event, and that you know that the problem is their's. If you don't check, you may discover that something which you regard as a high-priority item is not quite as high on their list.

It is your job to remind people of what is important. You can reinforce the notion of where they should direct their energy. If you keep telling people "This is the main event and what I want you to work on," you will help them to understand what does matter, and what they can get fired for. Otherwise, you are liable to find yourself with deadlines missed, with important supplies

Take action to:
  Move project forward.
  Retire project.
  Kill it off.
Never foster procrastination.

Determine exactly what the employee's next move will be. Write this down and clarify what is expected.

Decide when the action is to be completed and obtain the employee's agreement.

Determine whether the employee is to advise you before or after taking action.

Avoid accumulating additional problems.

Keep in mind that your objective is to increase leverage while minimizing risks.

Figure 35. Delegation.

not ordered, with a project that needs to be redone because the intent was improperly interpreted, and with a building not ready on time.

When responsibility passes to new hands you can feel uneasy. You may assign a publication that you developed to a new supervisor. You reassign a favorite and important client to a subordinate or appoint a new division director to an organization that you ran happily for years. They have their own way of working. You may feel a twinge; jealousy is common. If your subordinates win awards, establish new sales records, and achieve productivity gains of 10% when you could only achieve 5%, they have only done their jobs. They have made you look great.

Nonetheless, it can hurt when they go off in a new direction or no longer ask for your advice. That merely frees you to aim for a bigger picture and new meaningful goals. Delegation doesn't free you. Your job changes to that of monitor. Your job is to be certain that the publication's standards of substance and literacy are met, that the customer is getting attention, that productivity and morale are high, and that turnover and absenteeism are kept low.

When a new administrator was appointed to a major regional theater, he tried to follow the steps of his predecessor. Despite his efforts, it seemed different. A crispness was gone. Something was wrong. A board member noted that the previous administrator had been a gifted nagger. He was always walking around and seemed to be everywhere. He would drop in on the costume shop, test the properties, adjust the lights, sit in on rehearsal, check the membership mail, straighten the lobby signs. He never said much, but he looked sharply at everything. He asked questions. When asked, he did offer suggestions on staging, musical effects, the way the play's theme was interpreted. When the effect was wrong, he nagged until it was right. He knew what everybody did. Everyone felt his presence, his involvement. Everything that he did contributed to the theater's total effect. He never detracted from good supervision. People were in charge of their own work. He kept focusing on the standards of the theater, and left it to the company to figure out how to do it. They respected his taste. He lifted them to a larger conception of the work.

Striving to see that bigger picture is never easy. The tools of such work include many small disciplines that are unimportant in themselves but add up to needed habits. Your resolve allows you to change and to achieve excellence. You still risk meeting new people who may be hostile, or take the chance that you may have joined an enterprise that will fail. It is easy to manage when things go well. When they don't you have a specific challenge—to remain positive and well-centered, to build strong daily habits that enable you to get and keep the oars clicking together. Your demeanor will be watched, your example followed, your standards become the organization's standard.

You can resolve to be a positive example. If you are seen some days as a wicked witch or warlock, the ripple effect in the organization is powerful. When a manager's words and actions demonstrate a lack of faith in the organization's prosperity, morale suffers. Negative behavior from the top dampens the positive effort essential for consistent excellence. Achieving productivity and quality improvement requires a positive mental attitude. It is hard to smile every day, but nothing else will do. If you don't say "Good morning," the day begins badly for everyone. You may not feel that the morning is good, but your feelings are irrelevant. Say "Good morning" and smile even when it hurts. If you can't sustain a positive attitude, leave for the day or lock yourself in the office. Should this be more than a momentary aberration, have a long, serious talk with your best friend, buy yourself a present, take a vacation, or have a checkup. Your positive behavior is necessary if you are going to pull everyone together and keep them believing that they can produce and achieve difficult but worthwhile results.

At times, no doubt, you will feel cantankerous and preoccupied with your own rights. It seems normal to be mistrustful of authority and often, to feel like an adversary of institutions. Bosses and their dealings are seldom seen as totally legitimate. Those who work for you probably share similar views. Victory only comes from your conveying a philosophy based on a profound understanding of where the energy is that needs to be tapped. Otherwise, you will be unable to overcome the inertial drag of your organization.

Knowing when you do your best work enables you to establish daily habits that suit you and your job. A manager who does her best work in the afternoon reserves that time for important issues. She reorders her priorities, then, and plans and takes action on major projects or difficult jobs. Her plan centers on ensuring that her day is not controlled by the telephone, unexpected meetings, and the mail. She groups her tasks and has learned to say, "I can't talk with you now but I can see you in half an hour." She says, "Tell him that I can call at eleven if that is all right." By assigning time in blocks, she has freed herself for creative effort and planning. This way her daily tasks are not lost in the shuffle. She spent months learning to say "No, I can't take that call now" or to tell her secretary to hold her telephone calls. Her boss made it harder by calling her frequently during the day. Her office is physically remote from his while his other directors are in the same building. Surmising that he was merely curious and interested, she calls him early in the morning, and casually informs him of her day's activities. Then she can put her attention to her goals and plans, tour the shop to see how the work is going, and take care of pressing actions and necessary activities.

The telephone exercises a terrible tyranny on most of us. In an experiment at the New York World's Fair, anthropologist Edmund Carpenter dialed the pay phones. People going by, although they could not know who would be calling, answered the telephone. In another incident, a reporter learned the telephone number of the room in which a sniper had barricaded himself. The sniper answered the telephone to say, "I'm busy." When the telephone rings, most of us feel that we have to answer it.

Planning calls can enable you to control more of your time and help you achieve your objectives. Similarly, you can plan short meetings with your key subordinates for reports on projects and to discuss priorities. When people come in haphazardly, they interfere with your ability to plan and focus. You could set up appointments for receiving reports on problem solving. You could hold office hours at the close of the day after you have completed your desk work.

When you are planning projects, you may benefit from the ideas of people on your staff. They may be able to see missing pieces of the puzzle. When you can't see the path clearly, you could instead jump ahead and vividly envision the project completed, the product in use, the factory operating in space, and the curtain rising on opening night. If you describe what you want to see at the conclusion of the project you can figure backward to see what has to be done. This enables you to

Set goals and subgoals.

Establish a useful structure.

Identify priorities and themes.

Determine various possible paths.

Establish steps that can lead to goal achievement.

When you prepare plans you will, of course, estimate how much is unknown and figure that unknown into your system. Life is full of imponderables and variables. Five and ten year plans bear little relation to reality. However, you can sense trends. Your "peripheral" vision can enable you to be aware of changes that you cannot see. This will allow you to be alert to opportunity and hazard. The better you learn to plan, the better your plans will be.

Establish written formats that provide order, simplicity, and elegance. Make rules about reports: their style, standards, and the point at which you want to be involved. Then, stick to your rules. Like having a place for everything, this simplifies decision making and can increase productivity. When reports are due, limit your own role to checking substance against policy and to being certain that material is on target. If you must edit, limit yourself to clutter cutting. Don't rewrite the report yourself. If you are unhappy with the work, send it back to be rewritten. If you have clear, simple rules about such routine procedures as report writing, you can improve both quality and quantity. A manager who went to the training office for help came back with a simple format for proposals. The training office had quickly designed it using off-the-shelf materials from their "Writing Program for Managers." His people are all trained now to follow guidelines that allow them to concentrate on substance:

Objective.   Statement of problem to be solved or mission to be accomplished.

Recommendation.   What needs to be done and available options.

Rationale.   Why what you propose is the best choice.

Method.   Description of steps to achieve results.

Resources.   Expenses, people required and other costs including time.

He sets early deadlines until he has confidence that those working the problem have their eyes on the main event. He also requires that a one-page abstract be attached to any proposal of more than two pages. With great self-discipline, he has learned not to rewrite inadequate proposals. He has adapted a technique, attributed to Henry Kissinger, and merely writes on the cover: "Is this the best that you can do?"

Managers transferring problem-solving initiative from manager to subordinate are, in the phrase of Oncken and Wass, "getting rid of the monkeys on their backs." The "monkey" is the next move in the problem-solving process. The task is to transfer initiative to the subordinate and see that it stays there. To do this, you must always be certain that your subordinates have the initiative. "Boss, we've got a problem," implies an unworkable duality. You and your employee cannot have the monkey, the next move, astride both your backs. Your first step is, at a scheduled meeting with your employee, to figure out how the next move will be your subordinate's. Answers may elude you but the sight of the monkey leaving your office on your subordinate's back will be your reward. The next step is to give your subordinates no choice but to master "completed staff work." Each step in the process remains with the subordinate, but the action must never be allowed to become vague or indefinite. It is your job to monitor and review completed action, to maintain standards, and to encourage growth and excellence.

Since solving problems is not your main event, let your subordinates solve the problems. In most management training courses they teach managers to solve problems using the General

Electric method, the Dewey System or Kepner Tregoe, Synectics, morphological analysis, operations research, PERT, Osborne-Parnes, work simplification, or zero defects. These and all other problem-solving systems teach managers to look at the problem and to study causes, effects, possible actions, and to take and review action. The names and the number of steps vary. Synectics uses unlikely analogies to force innovation. In PERT, the task is to develop the critical, quickest, or most effective path to reach a solution. Operations research develops measurements from reason and experience and uses these measures for assessing efficiency and effectiveness.

When problem-solving is seen as important work and, therefore, the manager's job, both employees and managers expect managers to solve problems. Managers even take problems out of the hands of their subordinates because they believe that's what managers get paid to do.

In management training courses, they should teach managers how to teach problem-solving to their subordinates. This seldom happens. Instead, the manager treasures those techniques as if they were arcane secrets restricted to those of rank. If employees only knew, they would realize that there is nothing difficult or mysterious about problem-solving. They would be like Molière's Bourgeois Gentleman who discovered that he had been speaking prose all his life and had never even known it. We all solve problems. Some do it well. All of us could do it better. Techniques that become habits in problem-solving can lead to better performance.

In one major corporation a division kept losing money and neither technical expertise nor expensive management consultants were able to improve the situation. The company was reluctant to close the plant because the top manager's intuition told him that profit was possible. As a final step, the first-line supervisors were given a short course in work simplification. They were taught to "Find it, fix it, do it" (see Figure 36).

Then, all the workers were brought together with their supervisors. Top management instructed them to work out a method to improve both the operation and the product. Specifically, their task was to eliminate the deficit and to break even. They were left alone and kept full time on this project. In three days the lead supervisor announced that they had finished their problem-solving and were ready to work. They had made major changes in how the work was to be organized, how inspections and quality control were to be handled, and had greatly increased each worker's scope and responsibility. In effect, they had re-designed the operation. Within three months, the division was showing a modest profit. At that point, the chief executive officer went to the plant to congratulate the workers and to tell them to work out an even better solution. Assigned again to improve the methods and procedures, they worked for several days and de-vised new ways of working that caused their division to become a major factor in the company's success.

It was not magic. It was not easy. The people involved worked hard at finding ways to work effectively. On the job, they con-tinue to find better ways to do the work. That was ten years ago and they still periodically set time aside to renew their system and keep learning.

When problem-solving is regarded as management's job, em-ployees fill the manager's in-basket with problems. Then, they sit back and wait for solutions. If we think about it, the resident experts are those who do the work. If there are problems, they know about them. They should have an incentive to solve them.

Select the job to improve.
Get the facts.
Challenge the details.
List the possibilities.
Develop better methods.
Install improvements.

. . . Find it, fix it, do it. . . .

Figure 36. Work simplification.

The latest attempt to delegate problem-solving to workers is the Quality Circle, a major import, from Japan. Not surprisingly, the Japanese who visited America during the 1950s studied our concepts of management and quality control and implemented them with great success. Our ideas were then already well developed by such theorists as McGregor and Drucker, but few American managers were, or are, applying them.

A Quality Circle consists of a group of employees from a single work place and a supervisor who serves as leader. They voluntarily meet weekly on company time and on company premises for an hour to discuss, analyze, and propose solutions to specific quality problems. They first learn group communication processes, strategies for quality control, and the use of various measurement techniques. The leader is also trained in leadership skills, adult learning techniques, motivation, and communication. Circle leaders are cast in a participative management role, like Blake and Mouton's "9/9" manager, but try not to consciously alter their behavior.

They are taught to draw on the technical and personnel resources of the organization. They undertake to solve problems and maintain the quality of communication in the process. The Circle primarily monitors and measures change. More advanced Circles learn sampling, data arrangement, control charts, stratification, and scatter diagrams. The supervisor is able to develop concrete problem-solving, statistics, and measurement skills in the workers.

Nearly one-fourth of all Japanese hourly workers are members of Quality Circles. The overwhelming success of the technique should surprise no one. The concepts are sound and proven but almost no managers in this country have tried them. We have anachronistically insisted that the boss is the sole decision maker. The Japanese system emphasizes decision making by consensus and concern for the worker's well-being. William Ouchi says that this management approach is the key to Japanese success. It sounds so simple. As Theodore Levitt keeps reminding us, "The best way to manage is to keep it simple." Slightly more than one hundred American companies have organized Quality Circles. Lockheed, RCA, GE, GM, Martin Marietta, Westinghouse, and the Norfolk Naval Shipyard at Portsmouth, Virginia are among those trying it. They can tell you that it works.

Employees say that they like the Quality Circle approach because they find that managers are more likely to listen to suggestions from a circle whereas they might not listen to one or two people. When workers and supervisors have the incentive for solving their problems, productivity improvement and quality control become a way of life.

A lot of people figure that Quality Circles are another management fad, and they may be. It is mostly up to top management. Occasionally a maverick middle-manager will adapt zero-based budgeting, management by objectives, or job enrichment with startling success. The danger, then, is that the success itself may cause jealousy. This can result in other people destroying that success and messing up the manager's program. When this happens a lot of people suffer, the manager, his or her subordinates, the organization. Furthermore, others become afraid of taking risks and of taking action. This only underscores the need for top management to put emphasis on what really matters at work.

When you give up solving problems that subordinates could do, you will have time to do what counts. You could consider the hidden agendas, ask what is going on and what should be going on. If you deftly ask your subordinates this at staff meetings, you will acquire a reputation for getting to the heart of the matter.

If you give up problem-solving, you also have time to find answers and solutions to the major challenges of your organization. Your tours and observations of the workplace and your concentration on what is going on around you are the major tools in this activity. You ask yourself:

What am I doing?
> *How am I promoting excellence?*
> *What are we doing about productivity?*

What could I do?
> *How could I clarify the importance of excellence?*
> *Who could be enlisted in this cause?*

What should I do?
> *What do my goals demand that I do?*
> *What should others do?*

What might I do?
> *What structure might support positive results?*
> *What strategies might prove to be the means to positive ends?*

These are the same questions that you ask to determine what values, themes, and goals matter to you. They are just as useful when you are looking at the means to achieve them and will help you to stay on target.

The main event is excellence. This requires self-respect, respect of others, and a lot of hard work. To achieve excellence, you have to know what it is. As Joan Didion says,

> To give formal dinners in the rain forest would be pointless did not the candlelight flickering on the liana call forth deeper, stronger disciplines, values instilled long before. It is a kind of ritual, helping us to remember who and what we are. In order to remember it, one must have known it.

A friend of mine, once asked to sum up what she had gotten from our college experience, said "In one word, standards." It is useful for managers to be clear about standards, what is important, and what people get fired for.

Every organization has unwritten requirements for success. Some are open and known. Some are kept hidden from almost everyone. You need to learn what these rules are. Otherwise, you may stumble and not know why. If you know why, you may still stumble, but you will know what tripped you. With that knowledge, you will do a better job of getting up and moving on. One man worked successfully in an organization whose unacknowledged theme was "Beat the competition and never trust the stranger." His sales program always topped the competition, his products were innovative, the quality of his work was outstanding. His costs remained low and his profits were high. Nonetheless, in a close ethnic family organization, he remained the outsider. Neither they nor he seemed to realize how they kept him out of the club. It was some time later before he knew what had happened. From another organization, he watched the division that he had built up wither until it was finally closed. It was incomprehensible to him, to those with whom he had worked and to his customers, but it happened. His experience is common.

Arrogance leads us to use up people like tissue, or to believe that we can afford merely to exchange parts that don't work or continue to recall dangerous products. Time is running out. Mediocrity is unforgivable.

You may need to eliminate conditions that cause others to be exploited, dominated, or passive. Surprisingly, many high-level managers overlook situations in which employees are ridiculed or treated poorly. Sexual harassment is often treated as a joke. Some supervisors ridicule low-level employees who already have low self-esteem. If their confidence is undermined by teasing or insults the result can be worse performance. No one wants to be pushed around. The feeling of having no control over the future contributes to people's low aspirations.

Praise keeps productivity and quality high. This works especially with those who do routine jobs over a long period of time. We all appreciate recognition. No one ever can get too much approval. Some say that praise is unnecessary because people are paid to do their jobs. Of course they are. If, however, they do work that needs doing, work that you are glad not be doing yourself, it is good business to let them know. *Please* and *thank you* are still magic words.

Technical competence is expected but is no compensation for human indifference. No test measures your success. We know that bigger is not always better. Being efficient is not synonymous with being effective. Some services are nice but unnecessary. Your attention must be on the best alternative. You may have to compromise. Compromise can make us uncomfortable. Compromise can, however, enable you to secure group action. Otherwise, you could find that no action is possible.

We fear that compromise will lead to disregard of principle, to action based on expediency. That fear is well-founded. People who deviate from principle once may more easily do it a second time. When this happens with our leaders, we become nervous. We don't want leaders to be bought. They are supposed to stand for something.

Some leaders keep a "conscience" on the staff, an idealist, who reminds everyone of the importance of principle. Should you follow such a path, reward the "conscience" regularly and often. Choices in organizations are chancy and complex. We all know that the messengers who brought bad news, in supposedly more barbaric times, were often killed. It still happens. The "conscience" has a hard time, too, and needs your support.

The clarity of your objectives enables you to give each player a part, a job to do. You can concentrate on the dynamics, the changes, that are outside of your control. If you are alert to and appreciative of those in opposition, you may be able to counter their attacks. It is important that you be able to take action in adversity, to take off fast. The paradox is that while your decisiveness is essential, the self-confident and trustworthy leader is recognized by a lack of ready answers. We need, not certitude, but courage, and even, chivalry. We need allies.

For us to have allies and to work together in concert we need a code of behavior that works. Our lives are a series of meetings and greetings. Although we rely on experts to keep the machinery moving, good manners provide an important measure of leadership and defense against tyranny. The unwritten rules can be the basis of success. Your survival may depend upon your understanding of and adherence to the unwritten rules of your organization. They will vary from place to place but many organizations have codes that contain many elements in common:

Keep your eye on the main event.

The appearance of well-being, status, power, and prestige creates well-being, status, power, and prestige.

Commit yourself to excellence and expect it of others.

There is no such thing as a free ticket; every decision has both opportunity and cost.

Know how to do the necessary but unpleasant tasks.

Respect the talents of others.

The social area is important. Don't pass up opportunities.

Be generous but don't give something for nothing.

It never pays to make an enemy.

Tell the truth but don't tell everything.

Make your boss look great.

Keep personal affairs out of the office and don't talk about sex, age, or money.

Choose a field that you like, get training, learn everything.

What you say is more important than how you say it.

There will be other successes.

Move when you can't escape the knowledge that you have made a mistake.

If in doubt, listen to your stomach.

Happiness doesn't depend on your getting everything.

Establish a reputation for being on time, credible, and reliable.

Don't believe your own press.

The good opinion of your boss is more important than any objective excellence of performance.

High psychic energy is necessary.

Doing your job well is expected. Poor work carries disproportionate penalties.

Attention to goals and purposes pays off.

Serving splendidly is the reward. It is not rewarded.

Decisiveness is a good thing but give thought a chance.

Never work for a mean person.

Keep testing the variables.

Help as many people as you can.

Put on a happy face. Let your demeanor express confidence, optimism, and courage.

Whatever the unwritten rules where you work, knowing and acting on them can matter. With them under control, with the major theme, the mission, and the procedures clear, you can put your attention to those areas that have the biggest payoff. Some executives come to work asking where the money is. They concentrate their efforts on the products, services, and markets that produce or might produce the largest revenue. Others look for the greatest pain in the organization. Where pain is perceived, there is opportunity.

For productivity improvement to move from abstraction to reality, you will want to identify some particular targets where you can measure the results. Your sense of urgency can bring people together in a cooperative rather than an adversary relationship.

Doubt can be a powerful deterrent when you are developing new programs. Machiavelli remarked on the difficulty and danger in initiating a new order, and how doubtful it is that such an enterprise will be successful. Difficulty and danger can spur action. Doubt is different. Doubt may be a primary restraint. Doubt about the efficacy of an untried strategy or method stops people from even trying. Doubt leads to hesitation, rationalization, inertia, and inaction. People convince themselves that things are all right the way they are. If something was a good idea, someone would have done it already. People say that things don't need to be changed but merely need to be adjusted. In these times, however, any adjustment is so complicated that it really is a change.

When told that something is true, most of us look for flaws. We rub our hands gleefully when we find the error. Often, however, we begin with the assumption that something is false, when, in fact, it is true.

What is worse is that we act on that assumption. Hamlet claims that his father was murdered and no one believes him. Martha Mitchell says there was a cover-up, and people laugh. The employee group asking for a grievance committee is considered irresponsible. Studies affirm that women have abilities appropriate for management, but no one hires them. The achievement of a black man is seen as an aberration, an accident. The manager with bad news is branded as a troublemaker. The murder did take place. Corruption, unfair practices, and waste do exist. Nothing will cause an automatic signal to go off when you are about to make such an error.

Others will follow your lead. Your institutional behavior will be held up to as much moral accountability as your personal behavior. Should you make decisions that ignore human health or justice, your organization may do something with a great potential for destruction. If your action says that excellence is not practiced here, you should expect nothing more than mediocrity and poor workmanship. Only through your understanding of excellence, on a personal level, will your organization be able to make it a reality. It is all tied in with self-respect—individual and the collective self-respect of the organization. Some managers would be happier if personal integrity could be separated from institutional integrity. They would find it easier to live in a world with no institutional values—only personal ones. Such a world is chilling. When institutions see themselves as impersonal entities; the barbarian can take over. Mediocrity can win.

Winning itself causes problems. Most people associate winning with losing. They think that winning means going for the jugular. For the short term, you can win by being ruthless. It is seldom a good long-term strategy. People worry that others will see them as greedy, untrustworthy, and uncaring. Even worse, they may see *themselves* as greedy, untrustworthy, and uncaring of others. Most people, however, do better at not winning than winning. They don't exactly lose. The business of winning with grace is difficult. You want to win so that you think you are all right, and others think so, too. When you win, you should be certain that everybody else wins something. You can have what you want, but you can't have everything. Other people need something, too. Your happiness doesn't depend on your getting everything. Many rich and famous people spent their lives acquiring power and money. At the end, they wondered why they weren't loved, admired, and respected.

At the heart of excellence is your integrity. You will be trusted if you are able to fully integrate the whole organization, seeing the truth as clearly as possible and revealing only what the occasion requires. You often need help that no one can give you. You are thrust back on your own values, your judgment, your experience. You can learn from philosophy, history, and literature that your problems have all been faced before.

Managing on the downside of the economy, in a period of scarcity, is more common to the American experience than we, the children of affluence, are often aware. The American system of speed and economy invented by Eli Whitney was born of necessity. It was "the low state of the mechanik arts," to use his phrase, that caused him to move in the direction of interchangeable parts. Again and again agonizing work—not magic Yankee ingenuity—got us through the bad times. You can't be perfect. There are no miracles, no formulas to resolve confusion, no substitutes for clear thinking and hard work.

There is no right or best approach. For all your days, you will have to ask "Right for whom? Best for what purpose?" It won't get easier. It can get better. You can be a substantially different person, more likely to take risks at the right moment, better able to parry the attacks of others, to enlist others in your enterprises. When things aren't working, do something else.

We are a pragmatic people often acting as if what is true is what works. Therefore, we may believe that what works is what is true. We are also dreamers, often dangerous, open-eyed, dissatisfied, tinkering, looking-for-something-better dreamers. You can't learn to keep your eye on the main event between your first cup of coffee and dinnertime. You will never be finished. You are looking at a lifetime of work, but it might be worth the work of a lifetime. In your mind, somewhere, you may have an idea that has not yet worked. It may never work. It may look like a lost cause. It just may be true. Turning ideas into action could be worth the price. You could find that the attempt to achieve excellence at Chinese baseball is, indeed, the main event.

Bibliography

Adams, James L., *Conceptual Blockbusting*, New York: Norton, 1974.

Boettinger, Henry M., Is Management Really an Art?, *Harvard Business Review*, 75101, 1974.

Boettinger, Henry M., *Moving Mountains*, London: Macmillan, 1969.

Bolles, Richard Nelson, *What Color Is Your Parachute?*, Berkeley: Ten Speed Press, 1972.

Bostwick, Burdette E., *Resumé Writing*, New York: Wiley-Interscience, 1976.

Brilliant, Ashleigh, *I Have Abandoned My Search for Truth, and Am Now Looking for a Good Fantasy*, Santa Barbara: WoodBridge Press, 1980.

Brouwer, Paul J., The Power to See Ourselves, *Harvard Business Review*, 64602, 1964.

Cohen, Herb, *You Can Negotiate Anything*, Secaucus, N.J.: Lyle Stuart, 1980.

Crosby, Philip B., *The Art of Getting Your Own Sweet Way*, New York: McGraw-Hill, 1972.

Crystal, John C. & Richard N. Bolles, *Where Do I Go From Here With My Life?* New York: Seabury Press, 1974.

Culbert, Samuel A. & John J. MacDonough, *The Invisible War*, New York: Wiley, 1980.

Didion, Joan, *Slouching Toward Bethlehem*, New York: Simon & Schuster.

Djeddah, Eli, *Moving Up: How to Get High-Salaried Jobs*, Berkeley: Ten Speed Press, 1977.

Drucker, Peter F., *Management: Tasks, Responsibilities, Practices*, New York: Harper & Row, 1973.

Drucker, Peter F., *Men, Ideas, & Politics*, New York: Harper & Row, 1971.

Gardner, John W., How to Prevent Organizational Dry Rot, *Harper's Magazine*, October 1965.

Grinder, John & Richard Bandler, *The Structure of Magic II*, Palo Alto: Science and Behavior Books, 1976.

Haldane, Bernard, *How to Make a Habit of Success*, New York: Warner Books, 1979.

Herzberg, Frederick, One More Time: How Do You Motivate Employees?, *Harvard Business Review*, 68108, 1967.

Irish, Richard, *Go Hire Yourself an Employer*, New York: Anchor, 1973.

Ittelson, William H., *The AMES Demonstrations in Perception*, New York: Hafner, 1968.

Kanter, Rosabeth Moss, Power Failure in Management Circuits, *Harvard Business Review*, Vol. 57, 1979.

Kaufman, H.G., *Obsolescence and Professional Career Development*, New York: AMACOM, 1974.

Kellogg, Marion S., *Career Management*, New York: American Management Associations, 1972.

Levitt, Theodore, Marketing Myopia, *Harvard Business Review*, 75507, 1975.

Levitt, Theodore, Marketing When Things Change, *Harvard Business Review*, November–December 1977.

Lunding, F.J., G.L. Clements, & D.S. Perkins, Everyone Who Makes It Has a Mentor, *Harvard Business Review*, 78403, 1978.

McClelland, David C., *Power: The Inner Experience*, New York: Irvington Publishers, Wiley.

MacGregor, Douglas, *Human Side of Enterprise*, New York: McGraw-Hill, 1961.

Maier, Norman R.F., *Problem-Solving Discussions and Conferences: Leadership Method and Skills*, New York: McGraw-Hill, 1963.

May, Rollo, *Power & Innocence*, New York: Norton, 1963.

Mintzberg, Henry, The Manger's Job: Folklore and Fact, *Harvard Business Review*, 53:49–61, 1975.

Moreno, J.L., *Psychodrama*, Vol. I Beacon, N.Y. Beacon House, 1964.

Oncken, William Jr. & Donald L. Wass, Management Time: Who's Got the Monkey?, *Harvard Business Review*, 74607, 1974.

Ornstein, Robert E., *The Psychology of Consciousness*, New York: Viking, 1972.

Peters, Thomas J., Putting Excellence into Management, *Business Week*, July, 1980.

Postman, Neil & Charles Weingarter, *Teaching as a Subversive Activity*, New York: Delacorte Press, 1969.

Rogers, Carl R. & F.J. Roethlisberger, Barriers and Gateways to Communication, *Harvard Business Review*, 52408, 1952.

Rogers, Carl, *On Personal Power*, New York: Delta, 1978.

Siu, R.G.H., *The Craft of Power*, New York: Wiley, 1979.

Siu, R.G.H., *Transcending the Power Game*, New York: Wiley, 1980.

Stone, Janet & Jane Bachner, *Speaking Up*, New York: McGraw-Hill, 1977.

Terkel, Studs, *Working*, New York: Avon Publishers, 1976.

Trahey, Jane, *Jane Trahey on Woman and Power*, New York: Rawson Associates Publishers, 1978.

Weaver, Peter, *YOU, INC.*, New York: Doubleday, 1973.

Weisbord, Marvin R., What, Not Again! Manage People Better?, *Think* January–February 1970.

Work in America, Cambridge: MIT Press, 1973.

Zaleznik, Abraham, Managers and Leaders: Are They Different?, *Harvard Business Review*, May–June 1977.

Index